Ghost Towns of Michigan

Volume 1

LARRY WAKEFIELD

THUNDER BAY
— P R E S S —

Ghost Towns of Michigan Volume 1
©1994 by Larry Wakefield

Printed in the United States of America

ISBN 9781882376773

Cover design: Boreal Press, Haslett, Michigan

THUNDER BAY
—— P R E S S ——

Other Thunder Bay Press titles by Larry Wakefield
Ghost Towns of Michigan Volume 2
Ghost Towns of Michigan Volume 3

The photographs and illustrations in this book are attributed where the origin is known. The publisher and author apologize for any specific pictures we inadvertently may have used without permission.

For Lucille, of course

She always knew where I was,

because she was always with me.

Contents

Acknowledgments

I had help putting this book together. For historical material and photographs I am especially indebted to the following people:

Steve Harold, George Gregory and Ed Tillitson of Traverse City; Rena Bellinger and Phebe Cotton, Kalkaska; Betty Dunham, Sigma; Eleanor Bonner, Mancelona; David and Howard Moore, Peacock; Ray Nelson, Lucille O'Berg and Minnie Ringler, Chase; Joe Murphy, Grayling; Jenny Micinski, Baldwin; Orville Gillespie, Dublin; Randy Buyze, Westwood; Don Stedronski, Henry; Ed Belanger and Owen Bahle, Suttons Bay; Rita Remington Fiddes, Mary Manier, Larry Rice, Garnett Tripp and Tom Young, Big Rock; Ora E. Corriveau and Clarence O'Sullivan, Wilson; Harold and Marcia Bernhardt, Caspian; Mary Duvall, Lake City; Maxine Robinson and Harry Taylor, Harlan; Bernard S. Kondrat, Boyne Falls; Pat Dishaw, Mansfield; Rev. Orson

Deemer, Pauline Heyd, Jean Curtice Hutchins, Ren Briggs and Marjorie Smith, Dighton; Mary McNaughton, LeRoy; Harry Colony, St. Germaine, Wisconsin; and Laura Ashley, Michigan Department of State, History Division, Lansing.

All of these stories first appeared in the Summer Magazine of the Traverse City Record-Eagle, and I am grateful for permission to publish them here. Many thanks also to my Summer Magazine editors, Bob Kirk and Eileen Young, real professionals and fun to work with; and to Brian Steele, whose diagrammatic maps accompany each story and add much to its presentation.

Introductory Note

There are hundreds of ghost towns in Michigan. Most of them grew up along a railroad and around a sawmill or a mine. They flourished for a while, then languished and died when the timber was gone and the ore ran out and the railroad stopped running.

They range from lonesome sites where almost nothing is left to mark their former existence, to others where only a few crumbling houses and buildings remain. And there are others, too, where a few people still live, out of love, habit or necessity (and may resent someone calling their village a ghost town). These are ghost towns in the sense that now they are only pale apparitions of what they used to be. It is sometimes hard to draw the line between the quick and the dead.

If you are interested in once-upon-a-time, all ghost towns are interesting. Some are more interesting than others. Unlike Roy L. Dodge's excellent three-volume catalog of Michigan ghost towns, which lists well over a thousand of them, this book is exclusive, not inclusive. For this book I have chosen thirty-three of what I think are among the most interesting ghost towns in Michigan. The stories are written in a narrative style and form, and the treatment is in-depth.

My criteria for selecting them are: first, that enough good historic material and old photographs were available; second, that they have something that sets them apart from the common herd: a good yarn or two, interesting people. humor, an unusual origin and early development, a dramatic event, odd geographic or political features—in short, at least some of the ingredients for the making of a good narrative.

For I am a storyteller as well as a historian, and what is history but his story, her story, my story, your story? These stories are meant to entertain as well as to inform. I hope their readers will be interested enough to want to visit at least some of them and that knowing something about them in advance will increase their enjoyment.

At the same time, as a historian, I have been very careful with the facts. Behind each story are hours of painstaking research; talking with many people, reading old newspapers, old letters, old-timers' written recollections and family histories, courthouse records and other historical material. Each story is a distillation of heaps of such material. In each story I have tried to capture the essence, the flavor, the character of the place.

Finally, I want to say that it's been great fun meeting so many nice people and making so many new friends— so much fun, in fact, that there may be a second volume somewhere down the road.

1

A Railroad Stop Named Tunk

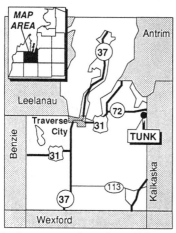

Several weeks ago, while browsing among the Michigan books at a local bookstore, I came across a new book on Michigan railroads. It's called *Along the Tracks: A Directory of Named Places on Michigan Railroads.* It was written by Graydon M. Meints and published in 1987 by the Clarke Historical Library at Central Michigan University.

Now, I am fascinated with railroads, but my interest in them is sentimental and historical rather than technical; I can't tell you, for example, if the screws on the engine fornistat have right- or left-hand threads, though some of my railroad-buff friends can, God bless 'em. So this kind of book is right down my alley.

Glancing through the place names in Grand Traverse County, I saw many ghost town names I recognized, names such as Mitchell, Westminster, and Angel, but I was intrigued by Tunk, which I had never heard of.

According to *Along the Tracks*, Tunk was on the Pere Marquette railroad about halfway between Mabel and Barker Creek. That would put it near the county line road, called Baggs Road, between Grand Traverse and Kalkaska counties.

I am so constituted that I must satisfy my curiosity about such things, if possible, or spend a lot more time on them than I should. So I called my friend Steve Harold, who is an historical museum director and consequently knows something about almost everything. But Tunk stumped him: he'd never heard the word except for a card game in which you say "tunk" and lay down your cards, hoping to catch your opponents with a fistful of big ones.

Then I called another friend, George Gregory, who knows more about Michigan railroads (including right- and left-hand fornistat screws) than anybody I know. He couldn't help me, either.

Finally I called a man who lives on Baggs Road, and he put me in touch with another man who not only remembers Tunk, he even knows how it got its name.

Ray Boyd grew up on a farm in eastern Grand Traverse County near Mabel. Its eighty acres are bisected north and south by Baggs Road, and were transsected east and west by the Pere Marquette railroad. Ray still owns the farm but lives now in Fife Lake, and he remembers Tunk very well.

It lay in the middle of the farm acreage about a quarter mile west of the Baggs Road crossing. It consisted of a side track, a hand-operated switch, a small shed for railroad tools, and a handcar, and really, that's about all. Ray remembers that as a boy he would watch the "stone trains" pass by as often as two or three times daily. In the early 1900s, the "stone trains" hauled huge quantities of limestone from a quarry in Petoskey. (I haven't been able to discover where the limestone went or what it was used for. My guess is that it went to southern Michigan cities on Lake Michigan for use in building breakwaters, cribs and piers. Another possibility is that it went to the big iron furnace in Muskegon—Campbell, Wyatt & Cannon—for use in smelting iron.)

It wasn't unusual, Ray says, to see southbound trains with as many as a hundred cars filled with limestone and with as many as three locomotives, two pulling and one pushing.

From the east end of Skekemog Lake, the trains had to climb a long, fairly steep grade to Barker Creek an beyond. There was no way that even three engines could haul more then thirty or forty linestone-laden cars up that long steep slope. So the crews would break the trains down into strings and the engines would haul up one string, sanding the rails for better traction as they went, deposit that string on the side track at Tunk, and

This is Tunk Today.

then go back for another. In railroad lingo that was called "doubling the hill."

Ray says that even then the loads were so heavy that the engines would be chattering with the strain as they neared the top of the hill. To the farm people who lived nearby it sounded like "tunk—tunk—tunk." And that, he says, is how Tunk got its name.

Nothing is left of Tunk today. The rails and the ties on this stretch of the Pere Marquette were taken up years ago. Long before that, the railroad men cut a deep ditch on each side of the main tracks, obscuring the side track. Like so many places where the railroad went—stations, switchyards, siding and whistle stops—Tunk now is only a memory.

Just a memory too, no doubt, is another railroad place in the book with an even zanier name than Tunk. It was on a south branch of the old Boyne City Railroad, and, so help me, it was called Goo.

2.
The Short,
Happy Life of Deward

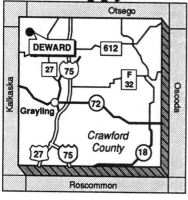

Deward, a lumbermill town in the northeastern corner of Crawford County, owed its name and its existence to David Ward. The curious thing is that it all happened after Ward was dead.

In many ways David Ward was an anomaly among Michigan's lumber kings. At 5'5½" and 145 pounds, he was a comparative midget beside such big men as R.G. Peters and Louis Sands of Manistee and Perry Hannah of Traverse City. Yet he was a human whirlwind—restless, tireless, physically as hard as nails.

Unlike most other lumbermen, he made his fortune not by cutting timber but by buying and selling large tracts of pine and hardwood to other northern Michigan lumbermen.

15

"I have no mills, furnaces, or great shows of business of any kind," he used to say. "I own the land, and those that want to develop it must come to me to buy. That's the kick." ("That's the kick" was one of his favorite expressions; it was always accompanied by a little kick of his foot.)

Born in 1822 in New York state, Ward was brought up on a farm in southern Michigan. He later taught school at Port Huron (Perry Hannah was one of his pupils), took a degree in medicine at the University of Michigan (but never practiced), and began his lumbering career as a surveyor and land looker in the great forests of north central Michigan. His fee was a quarter of the land he surveyed; and over the years he acquired some 220,000 acres of the finest white pine and hardwood in Crawford, Kalkaska, Antrim and Otsego counties.

Ward died in 1900. He was scarcely cold in his grave when his heirs began squabbling over his vast fortune. They wanted to liquidate the estate and get their money out as fast as possible. But the estate included a still untouched tract of timber at the headwaters of the Manistee River. It hadn't been cut because it was inaccessible: no railroad had yet penetrated the area and the rivers weren't deep enough to float the logs. Ward had estimated that it would take twenty years to log off the ninety thousand-acre tract.

The impatient heirs did it in ten.

First they imported the finest machinery from Germany and built a huge mill on the upper Manistee River, which they dammed for a millpond. Then they built a railroad into the heart of the timber from East Jordan to Frederic. They also built the town of Deward. It had a big boardinghouse, a company store, two rows of houses for two hundred families—but no saloon; as in most company milltowns, booze was forbidden (but the lumberjacks and millhands could buy it a few miles down the road at Frederic, and did, in great quantities). Lumber camps were established every two or three miles along the railroad. The great harvest began.

16

The great Deward sawmill.

Foundations of the old sawmill in 1960.

That mill was a wonder. It ran day and night, turning out two hundred thousand feet of lumber every twenty hours. Through a system of clutches, sections of the mill could be shut down for repair without closing down the whole operation. The record production for one year was fifty-two million board feet. That was more than half as much as Perry Hannah turned out in fifteen years at Traverse City.

The railroad carried the lumber to East Jordan at the rate of fifteen carloads a day. There it was loaded on barges and shipped to Chicago and from there all over the country. It is said that one entire year's production went to Argentina.

One giant white pine, named "The Great Monarch," produced 7,856 board feet of lumber, almost three-quarters of it better than common grade.

And then it was over—abruptly. When the timber was gone—in just ten years—the mill was dismantled and shipped away, and the town of Deward went out of existence. Hardly a trace of it remains today.

Many legends have come out of this fabulous lumber town. Joe Murphy, of Grayling, who grew up on a farm nearby, tells this story:

A man named Bert Demoth was paying attention to another Deward man's wife while her husband was away. The husband, Jim Carney, came home unexpectedly one day and took a shot at Bert with his pistol but missed. Demoth, more heavily armed, blew him away with a shotgun.

Demoth served several years in prison for his crime, and when he returned he would insist to anyone who would listen that he never should have been convicted of murder. It was a bad rap, he said.

"Anybody that pulls a pistol on a man with a shotgun—hell, that ain't murder," he said, "that's suicide."

Probably the funniest thing to come out of Deward was this letter:

Deward, Mich. May 8, 1903

Cleveland Saw Co.,
Cleveland, Ohio
Gentlemen:

I got a saw which I buy from you. By why for Gods sakes you doan send ne no handles? I loose to me my jobbing. Wants the use a saw when she doan got no handles? Sure thing you doan got no handles? Sure thing you doan treat me rite. I rote ten days and my boss he holler for logs like hell for

Abandoned stretch of the old Detroit and Charlevoix Railroad at Deward.

saw. You know it is plenty cold winter now. And the men no pull the saw, she got no handle so what the hell I go go to do with it? With them? With saw? Doan send me the handle pretty quick I goan send her back. I goan get some handle saw from Meyers Company, Good-by!

Yours truly,
Anthony "Push"

P.S. Since I rite you I find de goddam handle in the box. Excuse please.

3.

Sigma Started Late and Faded in the Stretch

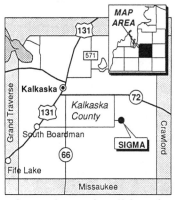

There's something surreal about Sigma. Take, for example, the name. Early Sigma was populated mostly by illiterate lumberjacks and mill hands, yet the village was named for a letter in the classic Greek alphabet. Whose idea was that?

It may have been the brainchild of William T. Kirkby, who became the first postmaster when Sigma was given a post office on May 13, 1914. If so, he must have resisted a natural temptation to call it Kirkby, because the post office was in his store. Afterward, it seemed a kind of anticlimax, because Sigma was almost entirely dependent on lumberjacks for its existence, and by 1914 the timber was almost gone. Hardscrabble farming kept it

The first Murphy Hotel at Sigma. *Betty J. Dunham Collection*

The second Murphy Hotel and Bice & Yeomans general store. At center is a rest area covered with pine boughs. *Dunham Collection*

Kirkby Bros. general store on Dish Day. *Dunham Collection*

Pere Marquette engine at Sigma. *Edward Tillitson Collection*

alive for a few more years, but that, too, soon petered out.

In the late 1890's, Manistee lumberman Louis Sands built a logging railroad from Sharon on the Manistee River to a point about half a mile from where Sigma now stands. There he established a big lumber camp, known as Camp 3, and began logging on a grand scale. Remnants of the camp are still visible today, and so is the old railroad grade. When Sigma got started, they called the lumber camp "Old Sigma."

Sigma didn't really get its start until around 1910, when the Manistee & Northeastern Railroad built its river branch to Grayling, and a depot at Sigma. George Bice and Naldo Yeomans put up a store near the depot and sold groceries, some meat and dry goods. Later, Fred Narrin took over the store and lived upstairs with his family. Art Murphy built a hotel near the store and boarded lumberjacks and others who came in on the train. When it burned down he built another.

A year or so later, the Kirkby brothers, Bill, Claude and Al, built a big general store and houses for their families on the opposite side of the street. There was a farm implement store next to the grocery, and a dance hall on the second floor where Sunday school classes were sometimes held. There never was a church—Sigma wasn't much for religion.

The Kirkbys also built a potato warehouse along the tracks (the old foundations are still there) and somebody else put up a pickle factory. The local farmers contracted to grow the cucumbers, and the factory sorted them into three different sizes, pickled them in big wooden vats, and shipped them out on the railroad for processing.

Friday was Dish Day at Kirkby's. Every Friday morning the whole neighborhood would gather around the store, a drawing was held, and the lucky winner would take home a set of dishes for six.

Sigma came close to being destroyed by fire in the summer of 1915 or 1916. A big forest fire blew in from the southwest and almost surrounded the town. Women

Louis Sands named his locomotives after his three daughters; this one is the Mattie E. Sands.

Murphy Hotel and Bice & Yeomans store. *Dunham Collection*

and children were evacuated to open farmland with as many of their prized possessions as they could carry; but the men stayed behind to fight the fire as best they could with their limited means. A railroad engine waited on the track to take them out to safety if that proved necessary. But the wind shifted at the last minute and the town was saved without the loss of a single building. The townspeople called it a miracle.

One pregnant woman had a kettle of dandelion greens on the stove when the evacuation order came. It was the only thing in her house that she chose to save. When asked why she chose the dandelion greens, she said she really didn't know but it seemed like a good idea at the time.

Kalkaska County went dry around 1916, but the lumberjacks and others could get all the drinks they wanted by catching the afternoon train to Grayling, an hour or so away. According to Frances (Narrin) Ridgly, who lived with her parents in Sigma from 1914 to 1917, they would return next morning in pretty bad shape. After easing the pains of withdrawal with a bottle of Hinkly's Bone Liniment or lemon extract (alcohol content 80 percent) from the store, they'd sleep it off at the "sky hotel" across the tracks—or, as one old-timer so graphically put it—"lay in the shade of a bob-wire fence for three days."

Sigma lost its post office in the early 1920s. The Kirkbys closed their store, tore it down and moved away. Some people moved their houses away, some just moved and left them. The old Murphy Hotel, after standing empty for several years, was finally torn down. And that, for all practical purposes, was the end of Sigma.

4.
Train Wreck at Bond's Mill

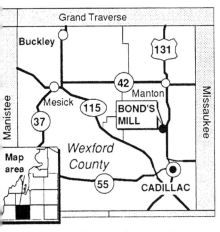

About the time William Mitchell and Jonathon Cobbs of Cobbs & Mitchell were building sawmills on Clam (now Cadillac) Lake in Wexford County, lumbermen Myron H. Bond and Frank Kyser were cutting timber for their mill on the newly arrived Grand Rapids & Indiana Railroad about six miles to the north.

Bond and Kyser built an earthen dam across the western end of a wetland and created a pond deep enough for washing and storing their logs. The pond is still known as Bond's Millpond. They built their mill in what is now a broad meadow just east of the pond.

The sawmill town known as Bond's Mill got a post office on October 30, 1872; Myron Bond was the first postmaster. He was succeeded by his partner Frank

Kyser, and the office operated until November 30, 1883. By that time, all the big timber around Bond's Mill was gone, and the mill itself was packed up and moved away. Now the only traces left of Bond's Mill are the earthen dam and the millpond.

One of the few memorable things about Bond's Mill is that it was the scene of a disastrous train wreck on the Grand Rapids & Indiana. It happened on September 22, 1901.

On that Sunday night, passenger train No. 15 was southbound with passengers from Petoskey and Traverse City. Freight train No. 35 was headed north; one of its cars was full of sheep. The excursion train naturally had the right of way, and the freight was scheduled to stop at Missaukee Junction and let it go through. So when engineer Fred Zimmerman failed to stop or even slow down at the junction, conductor Fred Volkert knew they were in big trouble.

The train wreck at Bond's Mill. *Grand Traverse Pioneer & Historical Society*

He climbed the ladder to the top of his caboose and raced along the tops of the cars to warn the engineer. Unfortunately, he was too late. The two trains came together on a curve with such force that the engines were virtually demolished, and the passenger train baggage car rode up and came down on top of the engine. The freight had been going about 30 mph, the passenger train about 45.

Engineer Zimmerman jumped with the other trainmen, but he was scalded by the steam from his ruptured engine's boiler and died a short time later. His brakeman, Hiram Witkop, was also fatally injured. D.F. Dark, engineer of the passenger train, suffered a broken arm. Other brakemen on both trains jumped to safety. None of the passengers was seriously injured, and only six sheep, in their car just behind the engine tender, were killed.

Conscious before he died, engineer Zimmerman shouldered the blame and told the trainmen that it was all because of his mistake, that he forgot to stop at Missaukee Junction.

5.

Wetzell: Broom Handles and a Bank Robbery

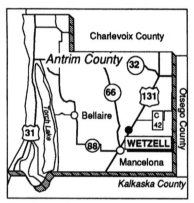

Wetzell, a ghost town on the Grand Rapids & Indiana Railroad between Mancelona and Alba in Antrim County, got its name in 1880 when the Wetzell brothers built a sawmill there and began cutting the pine and hemlock in the surrounding area. The GR&I had come through in 1872, but oddly enough, not until 1886, when most of the pine timber was gone, did Wetzell begin to flourish.

That year, Frank Harding, who had been employed for five years at the Mancelona Handle Company, organized the Wetzell Turning Works, which was soon to become one of the largest broom handle factories of the country.

Besides the big mill, 150 feet long and two stories high, Harding built the company town almost from scratch. It consisted of two store buildings, a school,

30

VILLAGE OF WETZELL

On November 10, 1881, the *Antrim County Herald* ran an advertisement about the village of Wetzell that read: "New Town. New Store. Everything New!" Earlier that year the Wetzell brothers had platted the village and opened a sawmill. As the town grew the pine forests were depleted. In 1886, Frank Harding changed Wetzell into a company town when he converted the sawmill into a wood turning factory that utilized the area's abundant hardwood forests. Harding attracted millhands to the town by guaranteeing them "steady work, good wages, free stove wood, free rent and water." Wetzell boomed, but its prosperity was fleeting. By 1909 timber supplies were low, the factory operated sporadically and Harding decided to cease operations. Without a new industry to sustain it, Wetzell became a ghost town.

Historic Site plaque at Wetzell.

Ruined foundations of the old hotel.

and more than fifty houses, rudely built but warm and comfortable. For his mill workers Harding sought sober and dependable married men with families, offering steady work at good pay, free housing, water and firewood. A boardinghouse was built by a man named Philo Beach; later it was operated by the Brown family, who installed a dance floor and roller-skating rink in the basement. The first church was built by Mennonites. Wetzell got its first post office on November 8, 1881, and one of the early postmasters was Frank Harding.

For something like twenty years, the Wetzell factory produced vast quantities of hardwood broom handles, croquet stakes and mallets and handles, carpet sweeper handles, and turnings for furniture and stairway banisters; they were shipped south on the GR&I to southern Michigan and to markets all over the country. It also supplied square pine timbers to shipbuilders in England for masts and spars.

Harding was a fair-minded but exacting employer. The town was strictly dry; no drinking was allowed. Mill hands who didn't conform to the rules were let go. Often the reason for discharging a man was simply Harding's judgment: "He spoils my system."

Fred Tomkins was brought up in Wetzell, worked at the mill for many years, and in old age wrote a memoir entitled "Ashes of the Years." One of the Wetzell stories he tells is of a one-armed worker at the mill named LaValley, who wore a hook on the other and was astonishingly dexterous with it. LaValley was fooling around one day with a hatchet in his hook-hand, whacking at a block of wood.

"Put your finger down here," he told Monte Latshaw, a fellow worker who happened to be passing by. "Put your finger down here and I'll chop it off for you."

So Latshaw put his finger down, thinking that LaValley was bluffing. LaValley struck with the hatchet, thinking that Latshaw would pull his finger away in time. Both were wrong, and Latshaw lost a finger.

The mill burned down in 1893 but was rebuilt immediately. It continued to operate at full blast until 1909, when it literally produced itself out of business; the hardwood was gone. The mill shut down, people moved away, the town lost its post office in 1910. By 1930 the population was down to 240.

Probably the most exciting thing ever to happen in the Wetzell area took place in that year, 1930, when four former Antrim County youths held up the bank at Mancelona. It was a typical depression-days bank holdup, complete with amateur bandits, local citizenry taking potshots at the fleeing robbers, and a chase by vigilantes reminiscent of the Keystone Cops. It would have been hilarious except that one innocent man was shot accidentally and crippled for life.

At 9:30 on Monday morning, June 2, the four men, all wearing masks, drove up to the bank in a Chevrolet sedan. Three of them entered the bank carrying shotguns, leaving a fourth to stand guard at the door. Inside, they ordered everybody up against the wall and started scooping up all the cash in sight. Hidden in a back

Old abandoned house at Wetzell.

room, however, one of the bank officers called the telephone operator and told her to sound the fire alarm.

Hearing the whistle, the robbers fled, jumped into their car, and roared out of town, closely followed by a posse of three men in another car, two of them riding the running boards. One of the robbers was grazed in the leg by a shot fired from a deer rifle by a clothing store clerk. The pursuers were ambushed by the bandits in hiding at the Wildfong farm near Wetzell. One posse man was wounded and their car was disabled. All scrambled for safety in a roadside ditch. The robbers jumped in their car and sped away.

Meanwhile, two other posses met north of Bellaire and blazed away at each other, each thinking that the other group was the bad guys. It was in this shoot-out, which lasted an hour, that Dr. John Grevers was wounded in the spine and crippled.

The robbers were rounded up a day or so later by state police and vigilantes. They were tried, convicted and sent to prison. The loot was a measly thousand dollars, most of which was recovered. Some bank robbers.

In 1988, mainly through the efforts of local historian Ernest Anger, Wetzell received a historical register designation from the state, and a large historical marker, clearly visible from nearby U.S. 131, was erected on the site. Except for two or three houses and the concrete foundations of the old hotel, it's about the only thing left of the town.

6.

Wilson Lingers On

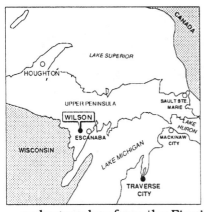

The old Wilson saloon is still open for business, and you can buy a drink—soft, hard or in-between—at the original mahogany bar from the Finnish barmaid or from one of the owners, Joyce and Clarence O'Sullivan, a genial Irish couple (except she's Lithuanian) who bought the place thirty years ago and live next door.

The bar itself is high off the floor. It's what they used to call a stand-up bar. The lumberjacks and millhands would "belly up" to the bar for their drinks. The way they figured it, bar stools were for sissies and loose women.

In these decadent times, however, there are tall bar stools for the clientele, which consists mainly of the pick-up truck trade. Business isn't rushing, but it's steady

Downtown Wilson in the early 1900s, Wilson saloon at center.

Wilson in the early 1900s.

The big Wilson sawmill was built in 1881.

Repairing the road-bed on the Green Bay, Escanaba
branch of the Chicago & Northwestern Railroad.

The old Enfield mansion today.

The Wilson depot.

and the O'Sullivans do all right. It's better in winter than summer, Joyce says, and better on rainy days than sunny, when there's nothing else to do.

Clarence says that the building hasn't changed a bit since it was built in 1902 by the Menominee Brewing Company, except maybe that the ceiling has been lowered a little. Back then, the ghost town of Wilson, on old U.S. 2 in Menominee County seventeen miles west of Escanaba, was already thirty years old.

In 1871, the Chicago & North Western Railroad came through Spalding Township on its way from Green Bay to Escanaba, and built a depot to serve the charcoal kilns at a little settlement the railroad called Ferry Switch. Other than the charcoal kilns there wasn't much to it, but the town came to life and started growing in 1881, when Frank D. Wilson built a big sawmill there. It got its first post office as Myra on February 24, 1881; and Daniel McIntyre, who built the first big general store, was its first postmaster. That same year the name was changed to Wilson, and the sawmill owner replaced the storekeeper as postmaster. The first school was built in 1881.

After that, the town grew by leaps and bounds, reaching a peak of more than four hundred people around 1910. In addition to the big sawmill, which specialized in cutting railroad ties, Wilson had a shingle mill, two general stores, a hotel, blacksmith shops, two saloons, and several cheese factories. One of its most impressive buildings, a two-story brick mansion, was built by August Enfield, owner of one of the general stores.

Wilson continued to flourish into the 1920s. Clarence O'Sullivan says that the second floor of the Wilson saloon was a dance hall. The finest dance bands from Wisconsin made it a must-stop on the polka circuit. People from miles around came to Wilson on Saturday nights and danced into the wee hours. Even as late as 1927, Wilson had a population of over four hundred.

Then things began to slide. The sawmill closed and the cheese factories went out of business. People moved away, looking for work. Fundamentally, Wilson had two strikes against it. One, it was too close to Escanaba and therefore unnecessary; two, it was on old U.S. 2 and thus practically invisible.

The C&NW trains still pass through Wilson but they don't stop any more. The old depot, discontinued in 1950, was moved away several years ago and now serves as a storage warehouse. Along with the saloon and two or three other empty buildings, the old Enfield mansion still stands, but its windows and doors are boarded up now, and the weeds and brush flourish like a jungle around it.

Wilson still has its post office; and you can still buy a drink—hard, soft or in-between—at the old Wilson saloon, the last and only business in town.

The Wilson saloon today.

7.

Idlewild: A Black Ghost Town

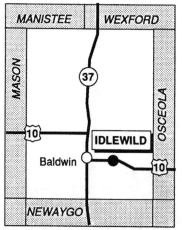

People who live there now are apt to take offense when Idlewild is called a ghost town. They say, "We're living here, aren't we? So how can you call it a ghost town when so many real live people are living in it?"

They have a point, no doubt about that. But when it comes right down to it, they must concede that the village now is only the merest shadow of what it used to be. So in that sense—not to put too fine a point on it—Idlewild is not only a ghost town, it's also the only black ghost town in Michigan.

Idlewild's population, like that of its close neighbor, Baldwin, is predominantly black. In the 1880s, many black families moved here to work on the railroad. Baldwin was an important junction of two branches of the Chicago & West Michigan Railroad. It was the place where the passenger trains picked up their Pullman cars and diners on the way to Detroit or Chicago, then dropped them off on the way back.

Black people were the Pullman porters, dining room attendants and cleaning women on the railroad. Even after passenger service was gone, many black families stayed on at Baldwin. Things were tough all over, but after all it was home, and for most blacks Baldwin was a better place to live than Detroit or Chicago.

Yet it wasn't the railroad that made Idlewild boom. Named after one of the five lakes in the area, Idlewild became a resort town, the biggest black summer resort in the country.

In 1910, it had a population of two. Two or three years later, four Chicago real estate men, all of them white, bought and platted twenty-seven hundred acres of wooded wilderness four miles east of Baldwin and began to promote "Idlewild Resort," a living and recreation community for Negroes. They mounted a high-powered advertising campaign, touting Idlewild as a wilderness paradise: "Beautiful lakes of pure spring water teeming with fish; high and dry building sites; game of all kinds roaming the green forests."

Actually, that wasn't too far from the truth. The lakes *were* (and are) spring-fed and beautiful. The fishing *was* good. The game *was* plentiful. For most city blacks, it was their first chance to enjoy a camping and summer resort experience, their first chance to see deer, bear, porcupines, raccoons, and other wildlife outside a zoo.

For just $35 ($6 down and $1 a week) they could buy a 25' x 100' lot, a piece of land to call their own. No wonder urban blacks bought them up like hotcakes.

And later, when such great black entertainers as Louis Armstrong and Aretha Franklin made Idlewild a stop on the "chittlin' circuit" and they could party all night at the Paradise Club or El Morocco, jiving till daylight and then clearing away the cobwebs with a dip in the lake—why, that was living, that was real value and then some for your money; nobody got shortchanged at Idlewild.

41

Abandoned cottage at Idlewild.

The hardware store went out of business years ago.

The celebrated black writer and educator, W. E. B. DuBois, who bought several lots at Idlewild, wrote that while he distrusted most real estate agents and all white real estate agents, he had to admit that the promoters had been fair. "They made money, but they haven't been hogs," he said. "Idlewild is worth every penny."

In the beginning, the promoters bussed hundreds of black people from Chicago, Cleveland and Detroit every summer weekend to look the place over. The only overnight accommodations then were rows of tents on wooden platforms on Williams Island at the north end of Lake Idlewild.

It wasn't long before houses and cottages began to spring up all around the lake. They ranged in size from tiny cabins (called "doghouses") to three-story mansions with wrought iron fences. A clubhouse for the residents was built on the island by the promoters; later it was turned into a dance pavilion and roller-skating rink.

Meanwhile, downtown Idlewild was booming, too. At its peak, the town had several hotels, grocery stores, restaurants and bars, a dime store, clothing store, hardware, dozens of stands selling "soul food" ribs, chicken and okra, and at least three nightclubs.

The great days of Idlewild were the late 1920s through the 1960s. It was estimated that on July 4, 1959, no fewer than twenty-five thousand people, both white and black, visited Idlewild. It was known then as the Las Vegas of Michigan. Among the star performers who played Idlewild were Fats Waller, Sarah Vaughn, Dinah Washington, Bill Cosby, Sammy Davis, Jr., Della Reese, T-Bone Walker and Jackie "Moms" Mabley. Many of them were still "on the way up".

"We could entertain anywhere," says the black proprietress of Idlewild's lone remaining store. "But we had to come here to be entertained."

Perhaps the most distinguished resident of Idlewild was Dr. Daniel H. Williams (after whom Williams Island was named), said to be the first surgeon in the nation to perform open-heart surgery.

There are still well-kept cottages on Lake Idlewild, but

Artist's rendition of the old Idlewild Club on Williams Island.

This Canadian puddingstone marks the spot where the pavilion stood.

most of the houses inland are deserted and falling apart. From a resort community, Idlewild has changed into a retirement community. Some of those who came here to play returned years later to stay.

Ironically, what killed Idlewild were the antidiscrimination laws of the 1950s and 1960s. For the first time ever, blacks now had access to places where formerly they were barred. Idlewild languished because blacks now had so many other choices.

Idlewild's great days are gone, but the memories linger on.

8.
Good Day at Big Rock

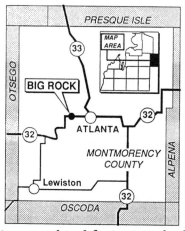

There's no question about how Big Rock, a ghost town in Montmorency County, got its name. Its most striking topographical feature is the huge granite boulder that lies on the village site at the corner of M-32 and Thornton Road. Like an iceberg, only the tip of it is showing, perhaps one-tenth. Yet the exposed surface measures about nine by twelve feet and stands a foot or two high. The rock must weigh somewhere between seventy-five and a hundred tons. It's big.

The rock bears some curious markings. They appear to be Indian moccasin footprints and the tracks of a deer; some people even see bear tracks. Early settlers speculated that these signs of a primitive chase were made while the stone was still soft, like clay, and that by some

46

quirk of nature the tracks were preserved when the clay metamorphosed into hard rock.

It's a pretty thought but bad geology. The boulder is obviously what geologists call a glacial erratic. They say it was formed several hundred millions of years ago—long before hominids or any other animals were around—and brought down from Canada by the glacier. Somebody's always trying to spoil the fun.

Big Rock is one of the oldest settlements in the county. The first white man to discover the big rock was a timber cruiser named Matthew King. The first settlers in the area were German immigrants Charles Meyer and August Barger, for whom Barger Creek was named. They had a hard time of it.

The first winter, on the point of starvation, they sent Meyer with the last halfloaf of bread to Otsego Lake, the nearest store and railroad stop. Meyer found a pile of rice that the mice had stolen, cleaned it up and fed the family for two days on it while he was gone. Barger and his wife came to the area with two daughters; Barger's wife died giving birth to twin daughters. Barger tried to raise the four daughters alone, but finally gave up, sold his farm to the Remington family and returned to Germany, writing back that one of his daughters had died on the way.

Other early settlers who carved farms out of the wilderness were the Maniers, Remingtons, Speisses and Rices. It was a wilderness teeming with wildlife: wolves, bears, lynx, deer and elk. One pioneer farmer is said to have amused himself by learning to howl like a wolf and raising a whole chorus of howling wolves at night in reply. (It's been seventy-five years or more since a wolf was seen in Montmorency County.)

Grocer Seth Gillett became Big Rock's first postmaster on March 22, 1882; the office was transferred to Atlanta that same year. In 1884, William H. Remington, who bought Gillett's store, secured a post office named Remington; it was renamed Big Rock on December 14, 1885. The office was discontinued in 1920.

Big Rock never got very big. At its peak about 1910,

Big Rock general store and school around 1900.
Montmorency County Historical Society.

Big Rock school and store around 1900.
Montmorency Historical Society.

Young woman with
bicycle on the big rock,
ca 1900. *Montmorency
Hist. Soc.*

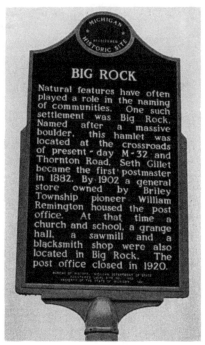

BIG ROCK

Natural features have often played a role in the naming of communities. One such settlement was Big Rock. Named after a massive boulder, this hamlet was located at the crossroads of present - day M - 32 and Thornton Road. Seth Gillet became the first postmaster in 1882. By 1902 a general store owned by Briley Township pioneer William Remington housed the post office. At that time a church and school, a grange hall, a sawmill and a blacksmith shop were also located in Big Rock. The post office closed in 1920.

Michigan Historic Site
plaque at Big Rock.

The big rock.

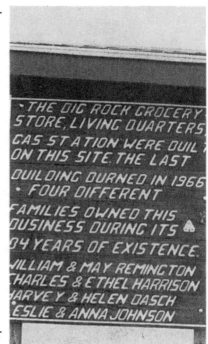

Historical marker
at Big Rock.

it had the general store, Grange Hall, machine shop, sawmill, school, church, and several houses—but only about two hundred people. In 1912, W. D. Rice, an itinerant preacher for the Assembly of God Church, horrified his wife Etta by cutting a hole in winter ice to baptize their daughter Grace. Fortunately, both mother and daughter survived.

According to a 1940 newspaper story, Charles Harrison, new owner of the general store, decided to dig up the rock (which lay just behind the store) and put it on display, possibly as a way of drumming up business. He dug a tunnel under it, but apparently that's as far as he got, for the story ends there.

Though in decline, Big Rock was still a lively community in the 1940s, when Big Rock women were still noted for the quality of their butter. One local man waxed poetic about it:

"The women of this place do not make the kind that looks as though it had been run through a honey

Store foundations at Big Rock today.

extractor, but good sweet gilt-edged butter that makes you think of green fields of clover, dotted with buttercups, and cool cellars with whitewashed walls; then that old butter bowl of Mother's, full of golden butter and the ladle standing upright in the center."

On May 25, 1991, thanks to the efforts of Mary Manier, Rita Remington Fiddes, and others, Big Rock was dedicated as a state historic site. Upwards of a hundred people, including many former residents from all over the county, were on hand to participate in the ceremonies.

The old Big Rock general store burned down on April 7, 1966. It was the first building in the village and almost the last one to go. Now all that's left of Big Rock is the church and the big rock.

9.

Aral: Ghost Town with a Bloody Past

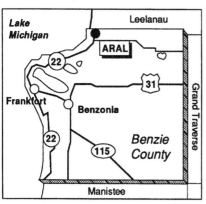

Aral, sometimes called Otter Creek, was a lumbermill town. It lay close to Lake Michigan in the northwest corner of Benzie County between Empire and Frankfort. It had a relatively short life, but among a multitude of similar ghost towns in northern lower Michigan, Aral has a special claim to distinction. In 1889, it was the scene of a brutal double murder that turned half the county into a lynch mob.

The area's first white settler was a printer and photographer named Robert Bancroft. After service in the Civil War he came north seeking peace and quiet. He found plenty of both for a while. After a few years, when homesteaders and loggers began to invade his privacy, he

Robert Bancroft's home at Aral.

Tombstone marks the grave of Neil Marshall in the Benzonia Cemetery.

Deputy sheriff Neil Marshall.

The "hanging tree" as it looks today.

House of David families; at right, the "hanging tree"

apparently decided to make the best of it and opened a general store.

In 1882, a Dr. Arthur O'Leary, who owned most of the land in Lake Township, built a sawmill on Otter Creek and began to harvest the great stands of white pine that grew along the lakeshore. The town of Aral grew up around the mill. By the mid-1880s it had a population of around two hundred—mostly mill hands and loggers, and their families—and consisted of several frame houses, two boardinghouses, the mill buildings, a general store and post office, and a camp for the Indian workers about a quarter mile to the south. The post office was named after the Aral Sea in Russia, which somebody suggested after two other names, Otter Creek and Bancroft, had been turned down by the postmaster general because Michigan already had post offices under those names.

In 1886, a Wisconsin lumberman, Charles T. Wright, leased the mill from O'Leary. By then most of the pine was gone, but Wright kept the mill busy turning out shingle bolts, fence posts, railroad ties, and hardwood for flooring and furniture, which he shipped across the lake to Kenosha in the company steam-powered barge.

Charley Wright was an attractive young man, but he had a streak of violence that surfaced when he was drinking. In 1889, he got into a dispute over taxes with the county authorities, and on August 10, Sheriff A. B. Case sent two of his deputies, Neil Marshall and Dr. Frank Thurber, with a writ of attachment for the logs at the Otter Creek mill.

Charley Wright met them there, armed with a rifle, a pistol and a snootful of whiskey. After a violent argument, Wright shot and killed both men, Marshall with the rifle, Thurber with the pistol. Then he disappeared into the woods.

Neil Marshall, reputedly at six-foot-six the biggest man in the county, was also one of the most popular. So, in popularity was Dr. Thurber. Word of the killings spread like wildfire and by late afternoon, a great crowd had gathered at the mill, coming in on horseback and afoot from all over the county. The mood was ugly. Their aim was to find Charley Wright and string him up. Someone had covered the two dead men with umbrellas where they lay in the dust, to protect them from the hot sun.

Wright was captured after one of his Indian workers, Lahala, revealed his hiding place under torture. Case hanged the poor fellow from a pine tree, instructing him to "shake his legs vigorously" when he was ready to talk—a not uncommon third-degree method in frontier towns in those days.

Case and his men spirited Wright away from the angry mob and took him by boat to Frankfort. Several months later, he was tried, convicted of two counts of murder in the first degree, and sentenced to life at Jackson prison, where, it was said, he became a great favorite of the warden, who let Wright drive his horse and carriage on errands and outings.

After Wright served only twelve years, Michigan Governor Hazen Pingree commuted his sentence to seventeen years; and with time off for good behavior, he was paroled in May 1902.

According to legend, Wright, on his way back to Wisconsin, stopped off at Aral and visited his former wife, who had divorced him while he was in prison and married a carpenter. She persuaded Wright, who had a beautiful baritone voice, to sing one of her favorite songs. Whereupon she fell weeping into his arms, and the carpenter, likewise affected, gave her back to Wright with his blessing. Anyhow, that's the story and it's all true, or ought to be. In any case, with or without his wife, Wright returned to Wisconsin, and except for one brief visit, was never seen in Michigan again.

Aral had a brief respite in 1908, when the mill was taken over by members of "King" Ben Purcell's House of David. By that time, the timber of all kinds had pretty much run out, and the bearded "Israelites" gave up around 1911 and moved back to Benton Harbor.

Aral dwindled after that. People died or drifted away. Other people ransacked and plundered the buildings for their white pine, said to be the finest wood in the world.

The last resident, Robert Bancroft's son Bertie, turned off the lights and closed the door on Aral forever in 1922.

All that remains are a few spiles of the old dock, the foundations of the Bancroft house and general store and of the old mill steam engine—and the hanging tree.

10
Dighton Has a Ghostly Charm

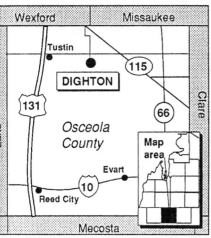

Dighton is a little ghost of a town in the green hills of northwestern Osceola County near the highest point in lower Michigan. The people who live there—the few who remain—say they have the best of both worlds: the peace and tranquility of nineteenth-century village life plus easy access, when they need it, to the frantic late-twentieth; downtown Cadillac is only twenty miles away. Seeing it today, you'd never guess that Dighton was once a rip-roaring logging town with a population of over a thousand.

The first settlement, which people now call Old Dighton, was a mile north and east of the present village. It consisted of a small store and post office, served by stage from Tustin, and a few scattered farms. Mary

59

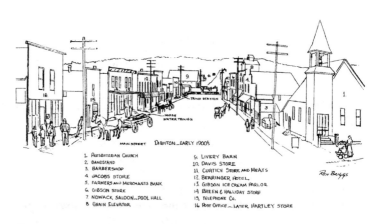

1. PRESBYTERIAN CHURCH
2. BANDSTAND
3. BARBERSHOP
4. JACOBS STORE
5. FARMERS AND MERCHANTS BANK
6. GIBSON STORE
7. NOWACK SALOON—POOL HALL
8. GRAIN ELEVATOR
9. LIVERY BARN
10. DAVIS STORE
11. CURTICE STORE AND MEATS
12. BERRINGER HOTEL
13. GIBSON ICE CREAM PARLOR
14. BREEN & HALLIDAY STORE
15. TELEPHONE CO.
16. POST OFFICE — LATER HARTLEY STORE

Downtown Dighton of 1908 in a painting and drawing by Dighton-born Ren Briggs.

The old Floyd Gibson store at Dighton.

The old Dighton school painted by Ren Briggs and today.

McNaughton, who at a zesty ninety is one of the oldest residents, remembers that her mother and father used to fill a milk pail with the ginseng roots they gathered in the woods and barter them for groceries at the store.

The new Dighton got started in 1901, when the Manistee & Grand Rapids Railroad (later called Michigan East & West) came through on its way to a rendezvous at Marion with the Toledo & Ann Arbor, having crossed the Grand Rapids & Indiana at Osceola Junction. The railroad was built to serve the needs of lumbermen Dennis Brothers of Grand Rapids, Cummer-Diggins of Cadillac, and Manistee's ubiquitous Louis Sands, who owned a piece of it. They were after the great stands of maple and beech for flooring and furniture.

Dighton grew up on both sides of the tracks, which neatly bisected the town. Its economy was fueled by three lumber mills employing hundreds of people. A man named Victor Rolfe, who came from Petoskey and was said to have Indian blood, built the first store. In the early days he was postmaster, freight agent, storekeeper and almost everything else combined; in fact, the railroad stop was first called Rolfe. Later, it was named after one of the area's earliest settlers, Dighton Marvin, whom everybody called "Dight."

Early Dighton was a pretty rowdy place. Marjorie Smith, who grew up there, tells this story: A young newcomer, Jared Nash, was walking down Main Street one evening when a man came crashing through a window in the dance hall above Steve Allen's store. He landed in a heap in the street and lay motionless. Jared waited awhile to see if anyone would come down to see about him, but nobody showed up. "There wasn't much law in Dighton in those days," Mrs. Smith says.

Some Dighton people, however, regarded dancing as immoral, to say nothing of drinking and throwing people out of second-story windows. When the Allen building mysteriously burned down one night, it was said that one of them might have had a hand in it, though nothing was ever proven.

Logging operations at Dighton around 1900 in a painting by
Ren Briggs; Dennis Brothers sawmill and gear-driven
Climax engine built in Detroit around 1890.

The favorite story of petite book-loving Jean Curtice Hutchins, whose grandfather owned the Curtice general store, is about a man who came up from the South to homestead a piece of land for farming. He expressed a desire to plant some apple trees, but the neighbors advised him against it. Dighton was so far north, they said, that the apples would ripen only on the south side.

Dighton's past had a dark side, too—one that people there would like to forget. It involved a crime of such ferocity that it troubles their dreams more than a century later.

A Negro named Daniel White came up from Big Rapids and took a homestead in the area, intending to bring up his family as soon as he could. One of the earliest settlers, Isaac Reames, objected simply because the man was black. Reames was a Civil War veteran who had fought on the Union side, but for some reason he hated blacks.

Reames persuaded his neighbor, young Jim Dagget, to help him do away with White. They enticed the black man into the woods on the pretext of locating a line stake, then murdered him, Dagget with a pistol, Reames with a knife. This was in November 1868.

When the body was discovered the following April and the evidence pointed to the two men, Reames talked Dagget into taking the rap. "I have a wife and family to support," Reames said. "You are young and single. You plead guilty and I will do my best to get you out."

Astonishingly, Dagget, who may have been somewhat simple-minded, went along with the plan. He was convicted of murder and served thirty- three years in Jackson prison. He was released in 1901, and it was said that Reames, now an old man, quaked with fear that Dagget would come looking for him. He died a short time later, after making a deathbed confession.

In 1914, the big flooring mill, Dighton's biggest employer at the time, burned down along with twenty four million feet of hardwood flooring. By then, the hardwood timber was about gone and the mill was never rebuilt. In 1920, the Dighton branch of the M&GR was abandoned and the tracks were taken up.

One old-timer lamented: "When the railroad came, we thought we had it made. But we didn't realize until later that it was only a rinky-dink, two-bit, little old pumpkin vine of a logging railroad."

Little remains of the village today. The old Davis family store, dating back to 1887, is still in operation, the only business in town. The Methodist church has been rebuilt; some people say they liked the old one better. Half a dozen rambling old houses still have occupants, including the rectory, the old Victor Rolfe house, and one of great charm that Jean Hutchins calls her 20-dollar house because her father paid that much for it during the depression. Dighton's back streets, once lined with mill workers' homes, are now overgrown with grass and weeds.

Downtown, across from the Davis store, stand two abandoned wooden buildings with high false fronts. Paintless but still intact, they look like a Hollywood set for a Western movie and somehow give the village much of its charm. Once upon a time, they were the Jacobs general store and the Gibson drugstore and telephone exchange.

11.
Jennings Got Moved Away

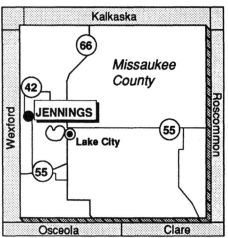

The now almost deserted hamlet of Jennings is said to be one of the two largest communities in Michigan to become a ghost town. The other is Au Sable, across the river from Oscoda.

Jennings lies on Crooked Lake, on the pine plains between Cadillac and Lake City. It started out as a lumber town, and lumbering is still the only activity that provides what life is left to the town today. But now, instead of virgin pine and hardwood, the descendants of the lumberjacks and mill hands cut popple and jackpine and scrub oak for firewood and paper making.

At its peak, roughly from 1885 to 1905, Jennings boasted a population of two thousand, a hotel, town hall, livery stable, saloon and pool hall, two general stores, a school, and four churches.

Jennings got its start in 1878 when William and James Dewings built a sawmill there and began cutting pine timber for several jobbers who set up camps in the area. The tiny settlement was then known as Crooked Lake. Later it was named Jennings after William Jennings Bryan or after a popular foreman at the mill—local historians aren't quite sure which.

Around 1882, two brother lumber barons, William and Austin Mitchell of Cadillac, bought the Dewings mill and enlarged it. They were said to be the first in Michigan (and maybe in the county) to introduce the double-cut band saw that doubled the speed of lumber production.

Six hundred men worked at the Mitchell mills, which operated six days a week, day and night, closing down at midnight on Saturdays. The Mitchells also had their own lumber camps. They were served by the Jennings & Northeastern Railroad, a branch of the Grand Rapids & Indiana, and miles and miles of narrow-gauge track with spurs reaching as far north into the woods as Kalkaska County. Besides the sawmills, there was a planing mill, a flooring mill and a shingle mill.

In the mid-1880s, the Cummer-Diggins Company of Cadillac built a huge chemical plant at Jennings. It processed tons of cordwood to make charcoal, wood alcohol, acetate of lime, and other wood by-products.

The timber finally ran out, and the town went into a rapid decline. By 1905, the population had dropped to five hundred.

Most of the people lived in houses owned by Mitchells, and in 1921 and 1922, a strange thing happened. The company moved seventy of the Jennings houses overland to Cadillac on trucks built specially for the purpose. The largest house, the home of the mill superintendent, had to be cut in two and carried one half at a time. Some of the houses still stand on Cadillac streets.

One of Jenning's oldest inhabitants at age 102, Maude Carson remembers the wild ride they had when their house was moved to Lake City. "The driver would signal with his horn when he was ready to start, and mother and I would brace ourselves in the corners of the living room," she says. "It was a wild ride but we saved a lot of things that might otherwise have got broken." Maude's mother owned her home; it wasn't a company house. Her father had been an engineer on the Jennings & Northeastern Railroad.

In the beginning, Jennings people were mostly Finns, who came to work in the mills. The lumberjacks, mostly Swedes and Norwegians, were the transients; they moved on when the timber was gone.

Oddly enough, though, there aren't many Finnish names in the two cemeteries at Jennings or among the people who live there now. That's because many of the Finns changed their names: Pisella became Peterson, Pausi became Hill. The reasons are somewhat obscure. Perhaps it was because the new names sounded a little less "foreign," a little easier to spell, a little easier to pronounce.

One of the eeriest places in Jennings is on the north side of town where the big Cummer-Diggins plant used to be. The plant was torn down in the early 1920s, and all that's left of it are the acres and acres of stubby con-

Planing mill and flooring plant at Jennings.

crete footings upon which the buildings used to stand. They look for all the world like a huge cutover forest of square grey stone stumps.

Here too are a number of steep-sided ravines running from the plant site to Crooked Lake a hundred yards or so away. During the depression of the 1930s, lean and hungry men dug them by hand to get at the big lead-pipe watermains that carried water to the mills from the lake.

They sold the lead pipe for scrap to help feed their families in those desperate days. Nobody objected.

The big sawmill shut down for good in 1922. It was torn down for its lumber, and the machinery was shipped to Sault Ste. Marie, where the Mitchells opened a new mill.

Now the wind blows through mostly empty streets where once stood the thriving town of Jennings, one of the two biggest ghost towns in Michigan.

12.

Henry: Where the Railroads Crossed

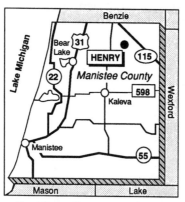

Henry, in northern Manistee County, now has a population of two. Which is quite a comedown when you consider that less than a century ago Henry was a railroad center, a booming town of several hundred people at the cross roads of three different railroads: the Pere Marquette, the Manistee & Northeastern, and the Arcadia & Betsey River. Henry is one of only four towns in the Grand Traverse region that had three railroads; the others are Copemish, Walton and Traverse City.

The first to arrive was Pere Marquette, in 1889. It was called the Chicago & West Michigan then; later it became the Chesapeake & Ohio. Its arrival didn't do much for Henry; not until seven years later did the town suddenly spring into existence. In 1895, Henry Starke completed

70

his 17-mile standard gauge railroad from Arcadia to Henry. He also built a big sawmill at Henry, and the town, named after him, grew up around the sawmill and the railroad depot. Henry got its third railroad in the late 1890s, when the Manistee & Northeastern completed its branch line from Lemon Lake to Henry.

Henry Starke was an interesting man. A German immigrant, he came to Michigan north woods from Milwaukee, where he'd been a construction contractor for building bridges, harbors, and piers. After opening a channel between Bar Lake and Lake Michigan, he built a sawmill at Arcadia and began cutting timber and shipping the lumber on schooners to Chicago and Milwaukee. Later, his Arcadia & Betsey River Railroad, with its link to the Pere Marquette at Henry, enabled him to ship his lumber year-round by rail.

At its peak in the early 1900s, Henry was the largest business district in Springdale Township. Besides the depot, it had a post office, a school, three stores, a hotel, and a large hall used for roller-skating and dancing. The stores were owned by Frank Burke, Riley Rensburger and C. M. Cushaway. Railroad agend David R. Rensburger became the town's first postmaster on February 12, 1902.

As in so many northern Michigan towns, lumber was the only reason for Henry's existence and when it ran out, the town soon languished and died. By 1927 the population was down to twenty-five. The Arcadia & Betsey River Railroad went out of business in 1937; its rails and ties were torn up and sold. The M&NE soon followed it into oblivion, and the C&O branch went out of existence a few years later.

The only things left of the railroads at Henry are the railroad grades, pointing in most major directions of the compass. They come together and intersect across the road from Don Stedronsky's house.

Don Stedronsky and his nine-year-old daughter Corrina are the sole remaining inhabitants of Henry. The house they live in, remodeled and modernized over the years, was originally the general store built by Frank

Pere Marquette mile-marker at Henry: 140 mile to Grand Rapids.

Stedronsky house at Henry.

Logging train on the Arcadia & Betsey River railroad near Henry.

Burke in the late 1890s. Don grew up in the house, as did his father before him. It is the only house in Henry.

Don's father, Charles, who died recently, told him stories about the earlier days at Henry. Whenever he got in a row with his dad, his father said, he'd walk across the road and hop a freight for Chicago. That was when the trains, both passenger and freight, passed through Henry every few hours of the day and night. Chicago was where Don's father met his mother. He lived there for a while, then came back to live in the Henry house when Don's grandfater died.

The Stedronsky house lies on Glovers Lake Road southwest of Thompsville. Just recently, though, Don was instrumental in getting the name changed to Henry Road—just the final three-quarters-of-a-mile part of it that runs north and south past his house.

In his backyard Don has erected an old Pere Marquette mile marker, with the numerals 140.1. That's about the distance between Grand Rapids and Henry, after the Pere Marquette abandoned its tracks from Kaleva to Baldwin in 1954 and established a new route through Manistee over the old M&NE tracks.

Now Don is planning to put up other signs north and south of his house. They will say, "You are now leaving Henry" or "This is the end of Henry."

He's doing his best to save Henry from complete extinction.

13.

Hoxeyville Marches on

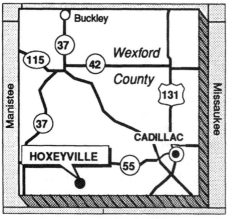

Hoxeyville, a ghost town in southwestern Wexford County, was first called Clay Hill for reasons that may have seemed obvious to people then but are obscure today. Somewhere in the vicinity there must be a hill full of clay, but nobody now seems to know exactly where it is.

In 1891, the name was changed to Hoxeyville in honor of its first settler, Jobe Hoxie.

The few remaining residents of the village, which still has a post office, celebrated its centennial in 1970. For that occasion, Steve Corson of Luther built an exact replica on a scale of one inch to the foot, of Henderson House, the first inn at the settlement. With the help of his wife Virginia he worked from the only known photograph of the place. The model has traveled widely

74

around the country, including the Smithsonian Institute in Washington, and is on permanent display at the county historical museum in Cadillac.

Hoxeyville is the second oldest village in Wexford County, the oldest being Sherman, which was established in 1869. In 1870, Thomas Henderson built a huge inn and tavern on the Northport-Newaygo State Road, the first road to enter the county. The inn, later known as the Brant "Half Way House" (halfway between Newaygo and Northport), had twenty rooms with bunk beds to accommodate travelers by stagecoach, horseback and foot.

The road had been completed through Wexford County in the 1860s. It closely followed an Indian trail used for hundreds, perhaps even thousands, of years: travelers called it "The Trail." It bisected the county north and south, running straight as a string just six miles east of the county line. With only minor deviations it followed the township lines from Hoxeyville to Sherman, where a bridge over the Manistee River had been built in 1864.

The Henderson House, which also housed the first post office, with Thomas Henderson as postmaster, was host to a steady stream of travelers seeking their fortunes in the north country. It was strategically situated not only on the new state road but also at its intersection with the only good county road to Cadillac, then called Clam Lake. It is said that, besides having bunk beds piled up to the ceilings, the inn also provided sleeping pallets in the attic to accommodate the overflow.

The town itself didn't really begin to flourish until 1889, when R. G. Peters built a branch line of his Manistee & Luther Railroad from Florence to Hoxeyville, a distance of about fifteen miles. Later it was extended to Olga Lake, where it hooked up with the Osceola branch of the Grand Rapids & Indiana; and still later, by another branch, almost to Cadillac.

Richard G. Peters of Manistee was a lumberman in the traditional flamboyant mold. A tall, lean, intense, and impatient sort of a man, he was forever in a hurry. His characteristic expression was: "Never mind talking about

R.G. Peters Salt and
Lumber Company
headquarters at
Hoxeyville in 1910.

Scale model of the
Henderson House
on display at the
Wexford County
Historical Museum.

High bridge on the Manistee & Luther railroad near Hoxeyville.

it, let's do it!" Besides the railroad, he owned a big sawmill and a salt mine in Manistee, and he was involved in a dozen other enterprises as well.

Peters built his railroad into Wexford County to harvest the remaining pockets of timber in South Branch, Henderson and Cherry Grove townships. The Pine River flowed through most of his timber holdings, but he didn't use it to transport his logs; he used the railroad. It had six engines, 250 cars, and employed 140 men.

Hoxeyville became the headquarters for the R. G. Peters Salt & Lumber Company's lumbering operations in the area. Here he built a big boardinghouse, barn, and office quarters, plus a railroad repair shop and a roundhouse. The Hoxeyville headquarters served some two dozen lumber camps in the immediate area.

Some of the buildings were destroyed by fire in 1913, and Peters abandoned the area. One of the few houses still in existence at Hoxeyville is said to be part of the men's shanty.

Stories about the legendary R. G. Peters are legion. One comes from Orval Gillespie, who was raised on a farm near Hoxeyville. The Hoxeyville branch of the M&L ran right through it, and Gillespie has memories of the trains passing day and night within a stone's throw of his house. He says he rode the train many times to Manistee and back before it finally gave up the ghost about 1920. All he had to do, he says, was step out the door and flag it down.

"It was a narrow-gauge railroad," he says, "and pretty rough in places. One day R. G. Peters was riding in the cab with the engineer and the fireman. The fireman was standing on the platform between the cab and coal tender, and when the train hit a rough place and lurched, it threw him off into the brush. He picked himself up unhurt and ran after the train as the engineer prepared to stop.

"But Peters said no. 'Never mind that guy," he told the engineer. 'If he hasn't got sense enough to hang on when he's riding a train, he deserves what he gets. Let him hoof it.'"

So on they went, Gillespie says. But pretty soon Peters changed his mind. "Wait a minute," he said. "Stop the train. We gotta go back and pick him up. He's the only guy we've got to shovel coal, because I sure as hell ain't gonna do it."

14.
The Ghostly Ruins of Marlborough

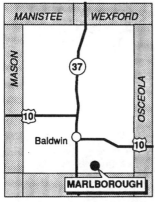

It's a spooky kind of place. Suddenly, walking down a quiet forest path, you stumble upon the vast ruins of what looks like an ancient lost city in the jungles of Sumatra or Yucatán.

There are massive concrete walls, three feet thick and thirty feet tall, some of them arched like Roman aquaducts; enormous brick-lined caverns (but most of the bricks are gone, pilfered over the years); and basement areas the size of two football fields. Before the sassafras and the poplars grew tall enough to hide them, the natives called this place "the Ruins of Rome."

What makes it even spookier are the booby traps; the place is full of them: hidden tunnels, sheer concrete cliffs, open holes with a drop of twenty feet to a cement

Some of the Marlborough ruins look like Roman aquaducts.

Mouth of one of the many tunnels.

floor. Fall into one of those and it could be years before somebody finds you. Access to the place isn't forbidden, but visitors are warned that they enter at their own risk.

In the wooded wilderness of southern Lake County, two miles south of Baldwin and a quarter mile east of M-37, lie the ruins of what was said to be the largest cement plant in the world and the deserted ghost town of Marlborough around it. Marlborough went from boom to bust in just five years. It had the shortest life of any town of comparable size in Michigan.

In 1902, a group of investors formed the Great Northern Cement Company, with a capital stock of $4 million, and bought eight thousand acres of land in Lake and Newaygo counties. On the west side of North Lake they built a mammoth cement factory and the company town of Marlborough for its workers.

The scheme was to make cement by the so-called wet method, using the vast quantities of marl in the nearby lakes and marshes as a substitute for limestone. The company believed it could make quality cement more cheaply by eliminating the costly process of crushing limerock. It spent more than a million dollars building the plant. Tons of its own product went into the construction.

The plant covered forty acres. It consisted of fourteen grinding mills, nine drying kilns, a machine shop, boiler shop, blacksmith shop, pattern shop, and a huge storage warehouse. It had its own power plant, which generated almost a thousand kilowatts, and its own railroad, which connected with the Pere Marquette Railroad, only a mile away.

The plant began operating in 1902. Its workers came from Baldwin, Muskegon, Grand Rapids, and from all over the country. Indiana farmers were led to believe that by selling their land and investing in company stock, they could obtain good jobs. But, lacking necessary skills, they had to settle for menial ones.

A recently married Indiana girl wrote her husband: "I'm worried about you. Won't the Indians bother you? Do you carry a gun?"

He replied: "Set your mind at rest about the Indians. Yes, there are a few here but they all speak English. Sometimes they get a little mixed up with firewater but they do no harm."

Thirty Hungarians lived in one house. They worked on three shifts and slept in three.

Marlborough was a model village. According to a story in the *Grand Rapids Press* in 1907, "Each building is modern and homelike, each of different design. . . Seventy-two of these pretty little homes were put on commodious building lots. . . served with electric light and a municipal water supply."

The town also had an eighty-eight room, three-story hotel, a big general store with an opera house above it, its own post office, a grade school, and a twenty-piece brass band.

From 1903 to 1906 were Marlborough's golden years. Then things started to go wrong. The company had made a serious error: instead of being cheaper, dredging and refining the marl proved to be much more expensive than the conventional method. Marlborough's product couldn't compete on the open market.

In 1907, the company failed to meet it obligations and was forced into bankruptcy. Its assets were sold on the courthouse steps at Baldwin for eighty-five thousand dollars. The plant closed and the workers departed. Many of the houses were moved, in whole or part, to Baldwin, Muskegon and Ludington, where some are still in use.

The plant buildings were sold to a Flint wrecking company. It dynamited them to get at the scrap metal, which brought twelve hundred dollars. An additional five thousand dollars was raised by wrecking the hotel.

A last-ditch attempt was made to salvage something more by selling the land for farming. In a scam like that of salting a gold mine, a showcase field was heavily fertilized and grew cabbages as big as basketballs. Carloads of prospective buyers were brought in, but there were few suckers among them. Most of them knew that the soil around Marlborough was about as poor as any you could find in Michigan.

In 1920, somebody noted with amusement that hogs were grazing in the now empty streets of Marlborough, streets that still bear the proud names Washington, Frontenac and Lafayette Boulevard.

15.
Cleon Died
While Harlan Thrived

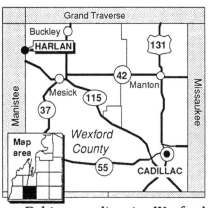

In the little ghost town of Harlan, the Robinsons and the Moores live just across the street from each other. Yet the Robinsons live in Wexford County, the Moores in Manistee County. How can that be?

Elementary, my dear Watson. It so happens that the Wexford-Manistee county line is the main street in Harlan.

It's been that way as long as anyone can remember, and it doesn't seem to have had any ill effects on the natives, among whom the incidence of split-personality disorder, for example, is no higher than anywhere else. Some people claim the local accent contains faint traces of a nasal prairie twang on the west side, and a flat Yankee drawl on the east, but others say that's nonsense.

84

The only difference, they say, is that some folks pay their taxes in Manistee County, others in Wexford. For most state matters, Harlan lies in Cleon Township in north-eastern Manistee County, a few mile southeast of Copemish. But its post office was in Wexford County.

The first settler in the area was Alex Pratt, who in 1857 drove a team of oxen all the way up from Benton Harbor. But it wasn't until 1889, when the Toledo Ann Arbor & Northern Railroad relocated its tracks, that Harlan came to life.

The railroad opened its line between Wexford and Manistee counties in 1888. Originally, it passed through the tiny settlement of Cleon, half a mile to the north. But it had difficulty keeping schedules on that route, which included a bad curve and an uphill grade to Copemish, and a year later it moved the tracks half a mile south. Former Cleon Township supervisor Harry Taylor, who operates a homestead farm nearby, still wonders about this.

"I always thought it was strange," he says, "that they would build three curves to eliminate one. But I guess they knew what they were doing."

Harlan prospered while Cleon withered away and disappeared. George Chubb built Harlan's first store in the fall of 1889, and the railroad put up a depot and section house at the same time. The place was first called Churchill's Siding, after a man named A. F. Churchill, who built a sawmill there and later bought the Chubb store. It was given a post office on March 31, 1890, and renamed for Harlan Caniff, who had looked after the mail in his home for several years. But the first official postmaster was Byron L. Deen.

As it grew, the town acquired another general store, another mill, a hotel, a blacksmith shop, a church, and a big new school, built in 1911. Along the tracks were a pickle factory and a potato storage warehouse. In 1912, the population was seventy-five.

August W. Wagner bought the store from Churchill in 1912, and he and his son Egbert ran it until it finally closed in 1959. Egbert's full name was Egbert Marcellus

The Wagner homestead and
family near Harlan. *Maxine
Robinson Collection.*

Jenny Wagner, Maxine
Robinson's aunt operated the
telephone exchange in the old
Wagner store. *Maxine Robinson.*

Abandoned Evangelical Church at Harlan.

Harlan School's first bus, built in 1923 by Emery Taylor.

Freak tree near Harlan.

The original Harlan depot is now a residence near Copemish.

Sargent Sand Company machinery on the railroad near Harlan.

Wagner; but he preferred to be called "Bert," and no wonder.

Bert's daughter, Maxine Robinson, born in Harlan as was her husband, Clarence, tells this story about her father. One day a woman came into the store with a crock of butter. She said a rat had got into it and wondered if she could exchange it for fresh.

"Sure," said Bert. He weighed it and disappeared into the back room. He reappeared with the butter, weighed it carefully, and gave it to the woman, who thanked him and departed beaming, a truly satisfied customer.

After she was gone, Bert's young clerk remonstrated with him. "How could you do such a thing? Give that woman fresh butter for something the rats had contaminated?"

"I didn't," Bert said. "She left here with the same butter she brought in."

Maxine says her father preferred farming to store keeping, but he did all right as a storekeeper, too.

Like many other northern Michigan villages, Harlan went into a steep decline during the depression years. The post office was closed in 1935, and the school in the 1950s, when area school districts were consolidated. The Evangelical Church, too, was abandoned about that time.

Harlan had a flurry of renewed activity in the 1970s, when the Sargent Sand Company of Saginaw built a plant for processing foundry sand on a railroad siding a mile east of town. It closed down when Ford Motor Company, its biggest customer, ceased operations at its Flat Rock, Michigan, foundry in 1982.

The plant and its rusting machinery still stands intact on the lonesome siding, and could become operational at short notice, it's said. But that's unlikely since Sargent operates a big sand-processing plant at Yuma that supplies all its present needs.

So Harlan has become a sleepy little ghost village of perhaps a dozen comfortable houses scattered along half a mile of quiet, tree-shaded country road that also happens to be the county line. The natives, far from being restless, say they like it that way.

16.

Onominee: An Indian Ghost Town

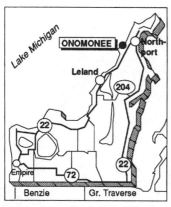

The old Indian village of Onominee (or Onominese) lies on a bluff overlooking Lake Michigan in Leelanau County about five miles north of Leland. Nothing is left of it now—nothing except a lonely Indian cemetery just south of where the village used to be. The cemetery, too, is invisible. Despite occasional efforts to keep it under control, the rank growth of underbrush has swallowed up the few headstones and crosses. Most of the graves are unmarked.

Yet here lie the remains of more than two hundred people. There are veterans of the Civil War and the Spanish-American War, scouts from the Indian wars, and soldiers in this bloody century's two great world wars. Most of them, though, are Indian men, women,

91

The meadow where Onominee village once lay.

Indian grave in Oniminee cemetery.

92

War veteran Joseph Wonageshick's grave at Onominee.

A small creek made this cut in the bluffs overlooking Lake Michigan where Onominee once stood.

and children whose names are now forgotten, who led peaceful lives and never fought in any war at all.

When the white men first came to the Grand Traverse region, they found three Indian settlements in what is now Leelanau County. Two villages were on the high bluff above Lake Michigan: an Ottawa camp called Cathead Village under Chief Nagonaba, which lay just north of today's Peterson Park; and another on the present site of Leland, whose leader was Chief Onominese; the Indians called it "Mishi-mi-go-bing," meaning "the place where the Indian canoes ran up the river because there was no harbor." This may originally have been an eastern outpost of the Menominee Indians, whose traditional homeland was directly across the lake in Wisconsin. The third settlement was a village of several Chippewa Indian families led by Chief Shabwasung and living on what is now Omena Point.

It should be understood that these were the semipermanent encampments of a nomadic people: summer camps. Like most sensible people, these Indians went south for the winter, hunting and fishing along the rivers of southern Michigan.

Onominese, Nagonaba, and their people usually wintered on or near the Black River in Allegan County and were well acquainted with the Reverend George N. Smith, who had done missionary work among the Indians there for ten years. So when Smith came north in 1848 to establish a new mission on Northport Bay, he easily persuaded the two Ottawa Indians bands to join him. He also persuaded Chief Onominese and his people to move farther north to Section 5 in Leelanau Township to be nearer the mission at Northport. And the move was made sometime between 1850 and 1855.

After the village was established, Reverend Smith came almost every Sunday to conduct Congregational church services there; he spoke fluent Ottawa-Chippewa and the Indians held him in high esteem. Later a small schoolhouse was built there, with three rooms for living quarters attached. The school opened in 1865, and Ann Craker Morgan, whose husband had died in the Civil

War, applied for and got the teaching job. From what her then eight-year old son, Norman, later wrote about it, one gathers that is wasn't altogether a pleasant experience.

"The experience and suffering that we endured in getting over there [from Northport] was one of the hardest trips I ever made through the woods. The location was about 3 miles southwest of Northport. There was not even the semblance of a road. A few blazed trees marked the trail, but it seemed as though those who did the blazing picked out the roughest ground they could find."

When they got there, Norman wrote, they were in almost as deep woods as those they had passed through. "But Old Lake Michigan was on one side of us and the house was located on the edge of the bank, which was nearly two hundred feet above the water and the bank was nearly perpendicular. Of all the wild places to try to exist, I don't believe a worse one could be found." Ann Morgan taught there for two years, until lonliness and isolation finally got her down. She had about twenty Indian pupils, ranging in age from seven to seventeen as near as anybody could tell.

Others wrote that the Indians lived like gypsies in bark-covered shelters and shacks in the surrounding woods. The children, they said, were like animals in the forest, lying down to sleep wherever they might be when night came. It was a far from an idyllic existence, but it suited the Indians just fine.

They could endure a lot of hardship, but they had no resistance to the white man's diseases. That's what finally did the village in. Its population was decimated by repeated epidemics of smallpox and dyptheria. The survivors scattered to the four winds—to isolated farms in the area and to the Indian villages of Peshawbestown and Cross Village.

Today there's a lovely green meadow where the village stood. A small creek runs through it. It was the waters of the creek that, over who knows how many years, eroded that great chasm in the bluff, at the edge of which the schoolhouse stood.

Now the wind off Lake Michigan blows waves in the tall meadow grass and rustles the leaves of the aspens in the old cemetery where most of the people who once lived at Onominee now lie buried.

(Onominee has several spellings: Onuminee, Onumunese, Onominese—take your pick. Early efforts to phoneticize Indian names into English often resulted in crude approximations of the original word.)

17.
Tragedy at the Mansfield Mine

During the twenty-some years of its existence, Mansfield, a little mining town in Iron County near Crystal Falls, probably never had a population of more than four hundred, even counting the dogs and cats. It had, nevertheless, one tragic claim to distinction. Mansfield was the scene of one of Michigan's worst mining disasters. It happened on the night of September 28, 1893.

In 1889, W. S. Calhoune discovered iron ore in profitable quantities there and platted the town. A year later, the Chicago & North Western Railroad built a branch line from Armenia Mine (near Crystal Falls) to the site and Mansfield Mining Company began developing the mine. The miners and their families represented a rich potpourri of ethnic backgrounds: Cornish, Italian,

Bridge across the Michigamme River at Mansfield; the large building at right center was the "dry", where miners prepared for shifts. *Mansfield Memories Committee.*

Mine disaster memorial.

James Corbett Saloon in Mansfield, 1903

Scandinavian, Finnish and Irish. The town soon acquired several boardinghouses, two general stores, three saloons and a school. Tom Corbett ran a stage line from Mansfield to Crystal Falls. John Erikson became the first postmaster on July 23, 1891.

By 1893, the Mansfield mine had six galleries at various levels, the deepest being 423 feet. All of them ran directly beneath, and parallel to, the Michigamme River. The top level was only thirty-five feet below the riverbed.

Five of the galleries had been stoped (mined out), leaving only the timber shoring and the pillars of ore to bear the tremendous weight of the earth above. The sixth and deepest level had not been stoped, and that's why twenty-one of the forty-eight miners who descended the shaft that fateful night escaped with their lives.

It is generally believed that the disaster occurred when the fifth level of the mine caved in, allowing the levels above, and consequently the river, to crash down on the miners.

Andrew Sullivan, night boss on the sixth level, heard the crash. He knew immediately what had happened and told his men to follow him to the ladder. The downdraft caused by the crash blew out their lanterns and candles, and they had to grope their way in total darkness to the shaft. All but four of them reached the ladder and started to climb.

At the fourth level they were met by a torrent of water from the Michigamme River, pouring down the shaft. From there they could hardly breathe except at the landings at each level, and reached safety at the top more dead than alive.

But alive. The miners on the fourth level weren't so lucky. Frank Rocco, night boss at the fourth level, was standing with another man when he heard the crash. Instead of heading for the skip (lift), which would have carried him to safety, he went back into the drift to warn his men, and was never seen again. Only the operator of the skip lived to tell the tale of his heroism.

Altogether, twenty-seven miners lost their lives. The death of so many husbands and fathers, as well as single men, was a terrible blow to the town, and it never recovered. By diverting the river into another channel, the mine was later redeemed and was operated until 1911 by the Oliver Mining Company. But by 1913, the mine was closed and Mansfield's post office was discontinued, and that was the end of Mansfield except as a ghost town.

Now all that marks the site are a bridge across the river, a few houses, and a gray granite monument that bears the names of twenty-seven miners who lost their lives in the Mansfield mine disaster.

18.
Isadore—and the Mystery of the Missing Nun

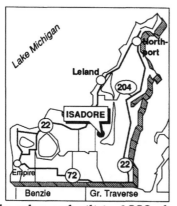

Unlike most other northern Michigan villages, Isadore grew up around a church, not a sawmill. Holy Rosary Catholic Church was built in 1883 almost entirely by the volunteer labor of the men of its parish. But what really put Isadore on the map was Michigan's most famous murder case.

Isadore, named after the patron saint of agriculture, was settled in the 1870s and 1880s mostly by immigrant Polish farmers. They'd got tired of Europe's interminable wars and fled their country to escape military conscription. They came late to Leelanau County, after much of the best land had been gobbled up by other ethnic groups, mainly French and German. But they were good farmers and husbandmen and prospered after a fashion.

At its peak Isadore never consisted of much more than the church, a school, a few nearby farmhouses, and a big general store owned and operated by the Rosinski family. Jacob Rosinski became its first postmaster in 1892, and the office operated until 1912, when it was removed to Cedar.

Holy Rosary Church is the religious, cultural and social center for its people. It christens them at birth, marries them when they wed, sustains them spiritually during the course of their lives, and when they die, tucks them away in the grassy church graveyard to sleep peacefully until the final trump.

Into this quiet, peaceful, pastoral community in 1907 came an almost unthinkable turn of events.

In 1906, a Felician nun, Sister Mary Janina, came north from the mother house in Detroit to teach in the church school—and for her health: she was slightly tubercular. A city girl born and bred, she nonetheless loved the outdoors. She took frequent walks in the nearby fields and woods and was sometimes late returning.

On Friday, August 23, 1907, she disappeared.

Her disappearance precipitated the biggest manhunt in Leelanau County's history. Hundreds of volunteers combed the fields, woods and swamps for miles around. A famous tracking dog was brought in. The sheriff and his deputies on horseback ran down every rumor, every clue. This went of for weeks, months, years. No trace of the nun was found.

Then, eight years later, in 1915, a woman confessed to a priest in Milwaukee that she had killed the nun and buried her body under the church. She was Stanislawa Lipczynska, who had been housekeeper for the parish priest, Father Edward Bieniawski, at the time of the nun's disappearance.

The church kept its secret for three years; then circumstances forced its hand. In 1918, it got word to the current priest at Isadore, Father Edward Podlaszewski, that he must disinter the nun's body and bury her in the church cemetery. Podlaszewski had plans to build a new church on the site of the old, and it was feared that the

Holy Rosary Church as it looked at the time of the murder.

The jailhouse at Leland, where the housekeeper was held before and during the trial.

The Rosinski house at Isadore.

The Rosinski house gutted by fire in 1989.

body would be discovered when the old wooden church was razed.

With the aid of his sexton, young Podlaszewski found the body and carried out his instructions.

A few months later, Podlaszewski told the story of the nun to his housekeeper, the daughter of a local farmer. She in turn told her father, who went to the sheriff—and the awful secret was out in the open at last.

In the most sensational trial in Leelanau County's history, Lipczynska was convicted of murder in the first degree. The trial was held at Leland in the fall of 1919. The housekeeper served seven years of a life sentence, was then pardoned by Governor Groesbeck, and spent her remaining years with her daughter near Milwaukee.

The new Holy Rosary Church, was built, as planned, in 1922. It has some of the most beautiful stained glass windows in the country. They were made by a German master craftsman and purchased for the church at a small fraction of their value, during Germany's terrible postwar inflation.

Today, besides the church buildings and the school, almost nothing is left of the village. One of its oldest landmarks, the Rosinski house and store, was gutted by fire in 1989.

19.
They Called It Jam One

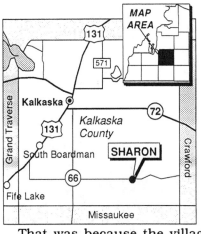

In the early days they called it Jam One—except the Swedes, who called it the Big Oley, meaning main stream. That was because the village of Sharon in southern Kalkaska County was the scene of the biggest logjam ever to occur on the Manistee River.

Sharon, now a ghost town, lies at the confluence of two rivers and a creek. The Manistee River and its North Branch and Cannon Creek all come together at Sharon. Both rivers were used in the early days to float pine logs down to the sawmills.

One spring day in the 1870s, all the banked logs on skidways along the North Branch near Sharon were unloaded all at once into the river. They came roaring down the Branch and smashed into the logs that already

Louis Sands' lumber Camp 25 near Sharon.

Pere Marquette Railroad handcar and water tower at Sharon.

filled the main stream. The result was a logjam that backed up the water in both rivers for miles and took the lumberjacks weeks to unscramble. It was, to borrow a current phrase, the mother of all logjams.

So the name was appropriate enough. But when Jam One's first settler, David C. Calkins, wrote to Lansing for a post office with that name, the postal authorities turned him down. Didn't like the name, they said, and enclosed a list of three others, including Sharon, which Calkins chose. It had a nice sound, he thought, soft, romantic and biblical—never mind that Jam One was anything but. Like Walton and other logging towns in the region, Jam One was a favorite hangout for lumberjacks. At one time there were twelve lumber camps in the area. The legendary Silver Jack Driscoll and another lumberjack from Dempsey's camp near Riverview once fought for one hour and forty-five minutes in Bill Peterson's saloon.

Calkins, a Civil War veteran, came to the area with his family in 1883 and settled on the west side of Cannon Creek, near the big bend in the Manistee River. Until the post office was established in 1891, mail for Jam One was delivered on horseback from Fletcher by a man named Chaney. George Johnson was Sharon's first postmaster.

Johnson, a cook at a small lumber camp nearby, married Calkins's daughter, Ella, and the two men teamed up to build Sharon's first hotel and livery stable. Later they parted company when Johnson built a saloon and a store. Calkins was opposed to drinking on religious grounds, and he sold his share of the properties to George and Ella.

Sharon became an important railroad junction in the 1890s. Manistee lumberman Louis Sands built a logging railroad from south of the river to Sharon and Sigma, and later on, farther north to the Blue Lake area. And in 1894, the Rapid City-Kalkaska branch of the Chicago & West Michigan (Pere Marquette) came through Sharon on its way to Stratford, where the Thayer Lumber Company of Ludington had begun cutting the big pine and hardwood timber in northeastern Missaukee County. Sharon soon became a boomtown of almost two thousand people—bigger than Kalkaska—with a thriving business district and six lumber mills.

In 1900, the Johnson store burned down; killing three men when the fire touched off a stored supply of dynamite. In a bizarre accident, the explosion drove a wood sliver through the stomach of Roy Dines, who was guarding his blacksmith shop from the spreading flames. He walked into his house, sat down behind his box stove and died. The two other men were burned to death.

After 1910, Sharon became quieter and more "respectable," and sparser in population; but it hadn't yet entirely shed its rough and rowdy ways. George Lisle Thayer, son of a boardinghouse keeper at Sharon, remembers fighting for three hours with Frank Birgy at a ball game there. Birgy won, and George said he never wanted to fight again as he was unable to milk cows for three weeks. "It was no wonder," George said, "the way he pounded my head."

Even as late as 1923, grocery store owner Ernest Tidd was shot and killed by a World War I veteran who claimed Tidd had defrauded him of some money. Tidd was famous for having used a logging chain to break up a free-for-all at John Gould's dance hall.

Just four miles south of Sharon was a railroad stop named Naples. Naples was a blueberry town. Every blueberry season a whole tent city of hundreds of people sprang up on Cannon Creek, where the blueberries grew in great abundance. The town even had its own makeshift barber shop, general store, and an open dance floor roofed with pine-tree boughs that everybody called The Bowery. Whole families lived in tents while harvesting the berries, which were picked up every day by the railroad and often filled half a boxcar. The pickers were paid sixty-five cents a crate, and sixty-five cents in those days would buy twenty-five pounds of flour.

But the timber finally ran out and the railroads died and the soil around Sharon was too poor to grow anything but one or two crops of potatoes. Sharon virtually came to an end when it lost its post office in 1921. Now nothing remains except the old abandoned schoolhouse. Built in the 1890s, it began with a kindergarten and ran through tenth grade.

Other ghost towns along the route of the Rapid City-Kalkaska-Stratford Railroad are Clearwater, Rugg, Mahan, Saunders, Eastman, Spencer, Sands, Halsted, Dempsey and Butcher. Kalkaska County has more ghost towns than any other county in the state. Ironically, it has only two villages of any size today.

20.
Murder at Sharon

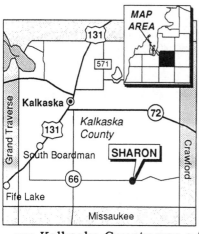

Like many other lumber towns in Michigan's early logging days, the village of Sharon on the Manistee River in southern Kalkaska County was a favorite watering hole for lumberjacks from miles around. Barroom fights were common—sometimes one-on-one, sometimes free-for-all—but so far as is known, no murder ever took place there until 1923, when the timber and the lumberjacks were long gone.

In 1923, Ernest F. Tidd was owner and proprietor of the big general store at Sharon. Fifteen years earlier he had taken over the stock of "The Irishman and the Jew" clothing store (which had its main store at Kalkaska) and later added groceries. He was also building a hotel, a lit-

111

tle at a time over the years, and hoped to open it soon. Tidd was a man of substance in the community.

He was also a man of violence, with a quick temper and an overbearing manner. He was famous for once having single-handedly broken up a free-for-all at John Gould's dance hall with a logging chain. Another story about him had it that when his pigs got into the garden

Old schoolhouse at Sharon.

Harry Stocking's soft drink stand in the early 1900s.

of a widow neighbor, and she complained, he turned her away with a few rough words—whereupon she shot the pigs. Not a nice man, Mr. Tidd—respected by some, feared by many, liked by only a few.

Tidd's sole employee at the store was a young man named Bruce Williams. Williams was a World War I veteran who had come to Sharon from somewhere out West and had been working for Tidd about three years. Upon his discharge from the army he had received a state bonus of three hundred dollars. This money he had loaned Tidd at 6 percent interest.

Lately, however, the two men had quarreled. Despite Williams's repeated requests for the money, Tidd had refused to pay—Tidd, sixty, patronized the young man and called him "boy." The quarrel came to a climax on July 25, 1923.

Tidd, Williams, and several others were in the store after supper on that Tuesday evening. Finally, everybody left except Tidd and Williams. Williams again asked Tidd for the money, but Tidd brushed him off with a curse. In a rage, Williams left the store, went to his shack and armed himself with a deer rifle. Then he waited in the shadows near the store for Tidd to close up. When Tidd finally emerged, he again demanded his money, and Tidd angrily refused. Williams then shot him just below the heart. Tidd fell to his knees and Williams pumped two more bullets into him. Then he turned and fled into the bush.

The coroner testified later that any one of the bullet wounds would have been fatal. Williams was a crack shot.

Williams was apprehended late Friday afternoon by Crawford County sheriff, Pete Jorgensen. He was found unarmed, wandering about in the pine plains near Portage Lake Junction. He seemed dazed and confused and offered no resistance. He couldn't remember his own name or where he was born. Since Tuesday night he had subsisted only on blueberries and a loaf of bread he'd bought at a house on the plains. He said he had returned to Sharon twice since the shooting but didn't know why. When told that Tidd was dead, he hung his head as though in grief but said nothing.

Williams was charged with first degree murder and went to trial in circuit court in September. There were no witnesses to the shooting but several testified about the quarrel over money. Others attested to Williams' good character and reliability.

"I'd take Williams home with me tonight," said Harry Stocking, a Kalkaska County farmer.

Williams himself took the stand and told about his war experiences and about Tidd's refusal to pay him the money he owed. He testified that Tidd had been abusive the first time he mentioned the matter back in May 1922. He admitted killing Tidd but pleaded extreme provocation.

The jury took a little more than four hours to reach a verdict of third degree manslaughter. Williams was sentenced to serve 7 to 15 years in the state penitentiary. It is said that he returned to the Sharon area after serving seven years and became a respected member of the community. The people of Sharon couldn't condone the killing, but many of them felt that Tidd had got what he deserved.

21.

Mabel Didn't Make It

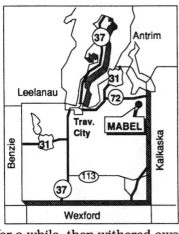

Mabel was typical of the many little towns in northern Michigan that sprang up along the railroads. They prospered for a while, then withered away and died.

Mabel was named for the daughter of Thomas T. Bates, pioneer Traverse City newspaper publisher. Bates bought the *Grand Traverse Herald* in 1876 from DeWitt C. Leach, who had bought it from the founder, Morgan Bates, in 1868.

The Chicago & West Michigan Railroad (later Pere Marquette and Chesapeake & Ohio) reached Traverse City in 1890, then pushed on to Charlevoix and Petoskey. Mabel got started in 1892, when Walter Hastings built a sawmill on the site, which lies on Mabel Road, two miles east of Williamsburg. That same year,

115

The wreck of the Pere Marquette train at Mabel.

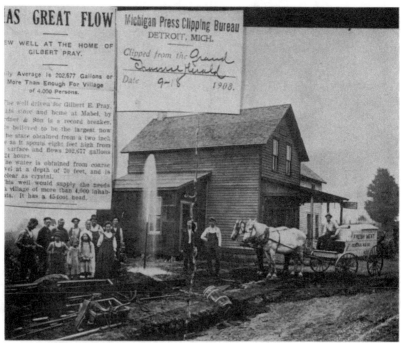

The artesian well, dug in 1908, was estimated at 202,677 gallons a day. *Grand Traverse Pioneer & Historical Society.*

The artesian well still flows at Mabel.

Welcoming sign on M-72 near Mabel.

the village showed enough promise and population to be awarded a post office; Adelbert Fairbanks was its first postmaster.

During the next few years, Mabel shipped large quantities of lumber, shingles, railroad ties, poles and potatoes to the outside world. At its peak, it had a sawmill, shingle mill, and a big general store.

By far the most exciting things that ever happened at

Mabel were a train wreck and a record-setting artesian well. The well came first.

In 1908, Gilbert Pray hired well drillers Gardener & Son to sink a well for his house and store. They hit artesian water at seventy feet, and it was a gusher. The water shot forty feet into the air, higher than the store building. Its flow was estimated at 202,677 gallons a day, enough to supply the needs of a village of more than four thousand people.

The well, said to be one of the largest in Michigan, made newspaper headlines all over the state. It had a forty-five-foot water head.

The train wreck happened a couple of years later. On the morning of July 19, 1910, two Pere Marquette freight trains came together near Mabel with such force that one engine was telescoped into the other. One man lost his life and five were injured in the accident.

One of the trains was an "extra," northbound from Traverse City. The other was the so-called stone train, hauling limestone from Petoskey. The stone train had been forced to "double the hill" northeast of Mabel, and after leaving the forward part of the train at Williamsburg, engine 160 went back with the caboose to pick up the rear end of it.

Both trains were running fast when they met on a blind curve half a mile from Mabel. Grover Hammond, a farmer who lived nearby, was standing on a hill where he could see both trains, though the engineer of each train couldn't see the other. He ran forward, shouting and waving his hat. Engineer Fred Vahey of the stone train saw him and shut off the steam. At almost the same instant, engineer Frank Griffin of the "extra" caught sight of the rapidly approaching danger and also shut down, slamming on the air brakes. Too late—the engines collided just seconds later.

Both engine crews managed to jump to safety before the crash. But brakeman Water Beeman of Elk Rapids, riding in the cab of the stone train, got caught in the wreckage and was killed. Slightly injured were engineer Vahey, brakeman Paul Obenauf, conductor Edward

Egan; and fireman George Jackson and conductor John Zimmerman, both of Traverse City. Cause of the accident: misinterpreted orders.

After that, Mabel resumed its gentle drift into the mists of history. The lumber petered out; the mill shut down. Mabel lost its post office in 1913, and the general store closed its doors soon after.

But the few people who live there now still call their home Mabel. And the artesian well still flows at a strong and steady rate, filling a pond in the open foundations of the old general store and a creek that meanders across the flat. And if you sit there by the water, in the shade of the giant willow tree, you can savor something of the slow time and quiet of a bygone way of life—even though on M-72, less than a quarter mile away, people in automobiles dash frantically by at seventy and eighty miles an hour, as if their lives depended on it.

22.

The Battle of Chase

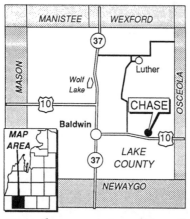

The citizens of Chase village were hopping mad. They said they'd never forgive their Baldwin neighbors. Even today, more than a century later, the few who are left will tell you—still with a trace of bitterness—how one night a gang of ruffians from Baldwin came down on the train and stole their courthouse. The story has been handed down from generation to generation. It happened in 1875.

The people of Chase in central Lake County trace its history back to when the village site was an Indian trading post in a trackless hardwood forest on a bend in the Pere Marquette River. Lorenzo Conklin, a farmer, became the first settler in 1862, but the town grew up from Charlie Joiner's sawmill, broom factory and shingle mill. It was first called Grendale, which by a clerical error in Lansing became Green Dell. Finally it was named Chase—after Abraham Lincoln's able but disloyal secretary of the treasury—when it was given a post office on March 29, 1872, with Alvin Joiner as postmaster. Chase is the oldest village in Lake County, and when the county was chartered in 1871, it became the county seat.

But not for long. The Baldwin people grew covetous of the courthouse and conspired (as the Chase people put it) to get it for themselves. In the election of April 1875, the question was put to the voters and Baldwin won out, 355 to 299. The Chase people immediately challenged the vote and called for an injunction, claiming that Baldwin had padded the voter registration rolls by putting up transients at the hotel and fraudulently registering their votes. They refused to turn over the court records to a delegation from Baldwin.

The delegation returned home empty-handed but angry and determined to get those records by force if necessary. They gathered reinforcements (some say from the saloons and the lumber camps) and on Saturday night, May 1, 1875, a group of sixty armed Baldwin men (the Chase people called it a mob) descended upon Chase village and the battle was joined. Reliable accounts are meager but as nearly as can be determined, here's what happened:

With the help of a man named Barney Riley, a conductor on the Flint & Pere Marquette Railroad, the vigilantes commandeered a locomotive and a flatcar and steamed down to Chase, ten miles away. They were armed to the teeth with crowbars, peaveys, hand spikes and broom handles.

The Chase people had gotten the word and were ready for them. They fought valiantly but, greatly outnumbered in a battle that lasted perhaps half an hour, were overwhelmed. The Baldwin people broke into a shed that housed a safe with the courthouse records, loaded it aboard the flatcar and took it back to Baldwin. Battle casualties numbered about twenty, and consisted mostly of bloody noses, multiple cuts and bruises and one broken collarbone. Thus ended the Battle of Chase.

Despite the loss of its courthouse, Chase continued to prosper as a logging and lumber center. It is said that

Climax engine at one of the sawmills at Chase around 1890.
Minnie Ringler Collection.

The old general store, built in 1914, still stands on U.S. 10 at
Chase. *Minnie Ringler.*

Construction of the general store in 1914.

This Chase roller mill was built in 1891, torn down in 1912. *Ringler.*

Chase was within earshot of the steam whistles of seventeen sawmills. It had its own newspaper, *The Eclipse*, two hotels, several general stores and blacksmith shops, two drugstores, two livery barns, a village waterworks and over a thousand people. Its business district is said to have extended for a mile on both sides of highway U.S. 10.

In 1892, however, it suffered a mortal blow. Fire destroyed all the buildings in town and all but one or two of the houses. The fire started in one of the drugstores in the late evening of April 26. Afterward, many Chase people called it arson and claimed they knew "who dun it." But they had no proof and the guilty party was never brought to justice.

Today there are only two commercial buildings on main street, and one is an antique shop, open only in the summer. Built in 1914, it housed a general store, post office and library, and an Odd Fellows Hall on the second floor. It is said to be one of the very few buildings of poured concrete still standing in northern Michigan. One old-timer says that the eight-inch-square tiers of concrete are hollow, but he doesn't know how that was accomplished in the pouring and building process.

Pere Marquette depot at Chase.

23.
Westwood Lives—Just Barely

Westwood, in northern Kalkaska County, recently increased its population by a whopping 50 percent. A married couple moved in across the road from the Buyze family, thus boosting the number of the town's inhabitants from four to six. Randy Buyze (pronounced "buys") says he hopes it won't create a traffic problem.

Randy and Mary Buyze and their two children live in the old Westwood schoolhouse. It was built in the 1870s, shortly after the village was platted on both sides of the Grand Rapids & Indiana Railroad, which reached Westwood in 1873. The Buyzes have completely remodeled the historic building into a comfortable home.

They own most of the town—what's left of it, including the church and school lots, the twenty-nine lots of Block

A, and the two village streets, Maple and Elm. Theirs is the only house still standing within the village limits. All the other houses and buildings were long ago torn down, destroyed by fire or moved to another site.

One summer several years ago, Randy and his son spent some time helping an antique collector locate and excavate all the old privies in town. The collector was after antique bottles, and he knew that old privies are among the best places to find them. In the old days, many people kept their patent medicine, tonic and whiskey bottles in the outhouse, (to hide the latter from their wives?), then dropped them down the hole when they were empty. Randy has an old plat map of the village, and he knew just where to look. The collector shared some of his bottle finds with Randy for his help.

Westwood, like many other northern Michigan villages, was largely the creation of one man. Canadian-born James Campbell came to the Westwood area, via California and the Washington territory, around 1869.

The old Westwood school is now a home.

He bought several hundred acres in Rapid River Township (the first township in the county to be organized) and built a general store about a mile from the present site of Westwood. Then, when the railroad came through, in 1873, he moved the store to the Westwood station, first called Havana. It was given a post office as Westwood in November of that year, and Campbell was its first postmaster.

In 1877, in partnership with William Duncan, D. Graham and C. M. Hall, Campbell built a sawmill at Westwood and platted the village. At its peak around 1900, Westwood, besides the sawmill and the general store, had a bowl factory, a hotel, and a blacksmith and wagon shop, a church and school, and several other stores. Over a hundred people, including twenty or more families, called it home.

The town began to decline soon after the turn of the century. It was gradually eclipsed by Mancelona, five miles to the north, which had become the business and industrial center of the area. A Kalkaska newspaper item dated September 10, 1914, noted that "Westwood is now without a store for the first time since it was founded."

Around 1915, an Ohio real estate company attempted to breathe new life into the community—and not incidentally to line its own pockets—by selling land in the area for farming and summer homes.

The Swigart Company bought hundreds of acres in the Starvation Lake area, just east of Westwood, and began to promote it, Florida-style. The company believed that "Starvation Lake" projected the wrong kind of image and changed the name to Star Lake. Legend has it that Starvation Lake got its name when an old trapper, sick and snowbound one savage winter, starved to death in his lonely cabin on the lake.

The company sold the land dirt cheap—but so was the soil. It was light, sandy, cutover timberland, worthless for farming and almost anything else. But the company salesmen were smart. They knew that at only one time of the year could they show the property with any hope of selling it: in the spring, when the young hardwoods were lush and green; at any other time they couldn't have given it away.

So, limiting their efforts to the spring and early summer, they bought the old Westwood Hotel and fixed it up as headquarters for wining and dining prospective customers whom they brought in by the trainload. Some of the more gullible victims bought property without even seeing it. The company did a land-office business until the bubble finally burst, leaving a lot of disillusioned people holding title to worthless real estate and Starvation Lake to its original and more appropriate name.

Probably the most exciting thing that ever happened at Westwood was a train wreck on the Pennsylvania Railroad. On September 2, 1916, a fast southbound passenger train hit a broken rail a mile and a half south of Westwood and derailed, seven of the passenger cars rolling down the high embankment. Many people were injured but only three of them seriously.

The whole town of Westwood and most of Mancelona turned out to view the wreckage and aid the injured. Doug Elder, of Mancelona, who rode out to the scene with his father, says he never saw so many horse-drawn buggies and wagons together in one place in his life.

Just a short distance away is the locale of Ernest Hemingway's wonderful story, "The Battler" in which Nick Adams has an encounter with a beat-up old prizefighter and his black companion in a jungle camp on the Rapid River along the tracks.

24.
North Unity Nearly Starved

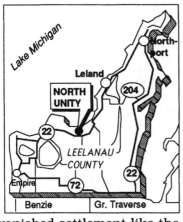

It was a near thing. If it hadn't been for some Indians and a few intrepid pioneers, North Unity might have become a vanished settlement like the "lost colony" on Roanoke Island in Virginia almost three centuries earlier.

North Unity, a ghost town in north central Leelanau County, was first settled in 1855 mostly by Czech immigrants. Several Czech and German families, after living a short while in Chicago, formed an association and delegated a few men to scout northern Lake Michigan in a sailboat for a suitable place to start a settlement. After some time on the lake, they docked at Good Harbor, a small village of French and Indians opposite the Manitou islands.

Frank Mikula's square-timbered cabin at North Unity.

Karel Rudolph's tombstone and carved likeness at the cemetery at North Unity.

From here they scouted along the shore to the west until they came to a beautiful, heavily wooded valley which was open to homesteading. It lay between Sugar Loaf hill (which they named "Blahnik" after a famous hill in their Bohemian homeland) and what is now known as Pyramid Point. This, they decided, was the ideal place for their settlement.

They reported their find back to Chicago, and in August 1855, several families decided to make the move. Along with a few Germans, they were the families of Anton Kucera, Charles Viskocil, Jacob Celak, Joseph Berkman, V. Jandus, Edward Kafka, N. Tabor, L. Kroupa, and two single men, Victor Petertyl and Albert Stephanek. Other families followed later in the fall. Almost all are well represented in the Grand Traverse region by their descendants today.

Back in 1855, there was just time enough, before winter set in, to clear a little land near the lakeshore and build a barracks, where all of them lived for a year or two until they could stake out homestead claims and build their own houses. The barracks was roughly 150 feet long by 20 feet wide, with rooms partitioned off for each family. The site was covered with huge pine and hemlock trees.

The first winter was long and hard. Only a few of the families had brought food supplies from Chicago, and there hadn't been time or space to put in gardens. Those who had extra food shared with the others until the supply ran out and everybody began to suffer from hunger.

To make matters worse, a schooner carrying food and other supplies from Chicago ran into a storm near the Manitou Islands, and the crew, presumably to lighten the load, jettisoned all the cargo except a barrel of whiskey on which they proceeded to get roaring drunk. The ship and crew survived, suffering nothing worse than hangovers, but that didn't help the starving settlers.

They managed to barter a little corn from the Indians, but nothing else was available. The lake froze early that winter, and no other boats could get through. Finally, on the point of starvation, Francis Kraits and Victor Musil with a few other men crossed the ice to North Manitou Island with a sled and brought back several bushels of potatoes. This sustained them until early spring when the passenger pigeons arrived and everybody with a gun turned out to shoot them. By then, too, the lakes had opened for fishing.

The village thrived during the next few years as more and more new people moved in. It had a schoolhouse, a sawmill, and a store. In 1859, it was awarded a post office, and John Hartung became its first postmaster. Joseph Shalda built a gristmill on the Lake Michigan outlet of the creek that bears his name. The village sent four men to fight for the Union in the Civil War. Two of them, Joseph Masopust and Matej Nemeskal, gave their lives for the cause.

But the settlement had a setback in 1871, when most of the village was destroyed by fire. After that, the villagers moved inland, and Shalda Corners, at the junction of M-22 and County Road 669, became the center of activity.

Anton Mikula's square-timbered cabin still stands in a field just west of Shalda Corners. The little house across the road was once the Shalda general store and home. It lies opposite the Cleveland Township Hall, where a bronze plaque on a huge glacial boulder commemorates the founding in 1855 of North Unity, home of many Leelanau County pioneers.

Nearby, in the old cemetery, the grim visage of Karel Rudolph, sculptured in stone and perched on the graveyard's tallest monument, gazes out over the site of his old hometown with a look of faint astonishment, as if he couldn't quite believe what's happened to the place.

A robin sometimes builds her nest in the opening on the opposite side.

25.
Fayette Awoke From Its Slumber

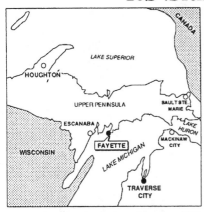

Like Deward and Stratford and dozens of other Michigan ghost towns, Fayette was a company town. The Jackson Iron Company of Negaunee built the town in 1867 and owned everything in it, including—so some of them said—the bodies and souls of its employees. Actually, the company, was a benevolent employer, paid good wages in gold, and took good care of its workers. Its product was pig iron.

Fayette, on Delta County's Garden Peninsula on Big Bay de Noc, was named for Fayette Brown, a company agent. He scouted the area in 1861 and reported that it offered an ideal location for iron smelting operations. It had abundant stands of hardwood for making charcoal, huge outcroppings of limestone for building material and

Fayette on Snail Shell Harbor.

The old hotel at Fayette.

Another view of Fayette on Snail Shell Harbor.

Pump and watering trough on the hotel grounds; author's wife Lucille.

Ruined wall of the old general store at Fayette.

flux for the furnaces, and a snug, deep-water harbor for shipping. Because of its shape, the beautiful little bay had been known for years to Great Lakes sailors as Snail Shell Harbor.

The company acquired the land, including some twenty thousand acres of hardwood forest, in 1864. The first furnace stack was built in 1867 of limestone blocks quarried from the harbor cliffs, and the first pig iron was produced in December of that year.

A second furnace was built in 1870. Iron ore was transported from the railhead at Escanaba by a tug and barges. The company built its own narrow-gauge railroad and hauled charcoal from its sets of bee-shaped brick kilns all over the lower part of the Garden Peninsula. Each set of kilns had its own boardinghouse and a group of log cabins for its workers.

During the 1870s and 1880s, Fayette became the second largest producer of quality charcoal-forged iron in Michigan. Altogether, it produced some 230,000 tons of pig iron. Most of it was shipped to Chicago.

Fayette boomed during the seventies and eighties. It got a post office in 1870; Marvin H. Brown, the company agent, was postmaster. At its peak in the late 1880s, Fayette had a general store, office building, superintendent's and supervisor's houses, a machine shop, blacksmith, doctor's office, hotel, boardinghouse, opera house, 40 log cabins for its workers and their families, and a population of five hundred—but no saloons.

By company decree the town was dry. However, it made an exception in the case of "Pig Iron" Fred Hink, one of its workers who had been disabled in a plant accident. He had been permitted to open a tavern about a mile from town on the Garden road. That led to trouble.

"Pig Iron" was a good guy, but his tavern became a hangout for a bunch of toughs known as the Summers Gang. Jim Summers operated a bordello known as the "The Stockade" a mile or two south of Fayette. It had a high wooden fence around it to keep the girls from leaving without permission—many of them had been forced into prostitution against their will.

Ruins of the blast furnaces.

Dr. C. N. Bellows house at Fayette.

Trouble started when one of the girls escaped and sought asylum at Fayette after wandering in the woods for two days. The story goes that she was taken in at the home of the deputy sheriff, but instead of protecting her he turned her over to Jim Summers, who was waiting outside in a buggy.

This aroused the citizens of Fayette to a fury. They held a town meeting, formed a posse of vigilantes, and, armed with clubs and mops and axe-handles, descended upon Pig Iron's tavern, where the Summers Gang was whooping it up. After beating up the gang, they marched to The Stockade, liberated the girls, and left Summers battered and bleeding on the beach to die. But when some of his friends returned next morning to bury him, the body had disappeared.

Fire destroyed the furnaces in 1883. They were rebuilt and smelting operations continued for a few years; but by that time the area's hardwood forests had been virtually wiped out for charcoal and new and more efficient methods of iron smelting were coming into use.

In 1959, after slumbering on Snail Shell Harbor for more than half a century, visited only by occasional travelers and boatmen, Fayette was acquired by the Michigan Department of Natural Resources and transformed into what many people consider Michigan's most interesting and beautiful state park. The castlelike ruins of the great blast furnaces have been left virtually untouched, but many of the frame buildings have been mended and completely restored. Many are now on-site museums, filled with antiques and memorabilia of their time. Fayette now is truly a long step back in time.

26.
Atkinson, Gibbs City, and Badman Jim Summers

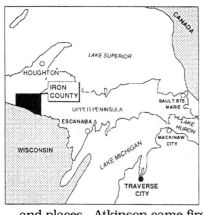

The thing to remember about Atkinson and Gibbs City is that they were essentially the same town at different times and places. Atkinson came first.

Around 1887, J. K. Stack, an Escanaba banker, and Henry M. Atkinson, from a Green Bay farm family, organized the Metropolitan Lumber Company and secured thousands of acres of virgin pine lumber along the north and south branches of the Paint River in north central Iron County. They dammed the river for a millpond and built a big sawmill on the north bank about a mile below the confluence of the two branches. Within a short time a good-sized town sprang up on the big flat near the mill. At its peak a few years later, the town had board side-

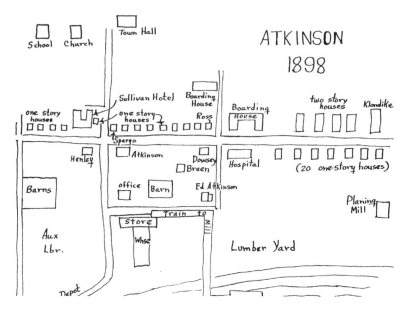

Street plan of Atkinson 1898. *Iron County Historical Museum.*

Gibbs City Boarding House. *Iron County Hist. Museum.*

Lumber company landing crew 1896.

Gibbs Camp locomotive.

This chimney of the old Ed Atkinson house is all that remains of Atkinson.

walks, electric lights, two hotels, a railroad depot on a branch of the Chicago & North Western Railroad, which terminated there, a hospital, and a big general store housing a library and a post office. Thomas G. Atkinson, secretary of the lumber company, was its first postmaster.

Meanwhile, the Atkinson area had become the scene of a homesteaders land rush. Settlers were attracted by the great pine forests and fertile land in the Paint River valley. But a dispute arose between the farmers and the lumber company, and soon it developed into a war like the one being waged out West between homesteaders and cattle ranchers.

There were acts of sabotage, violence and counterviolence. Mill saws were stripped of their teeth by the railroad spikes driven into pine trees by the homesteaders. Logging teams were shot and killed. One homesteader who claimed the forty acres on which the sawmill was built was found dead one morning, lying face down in three inches of water. The coroner, a company man, called it death by drowning.

One of the leaders of the homesteaders was the notorious Jim Summers, the same Jim Summers who had been left for dead on the beach near Fayette after a beating by the citizens of that town. (The story goes that he revived during the night and crossed Big Bay De Noc in a rowboat, never again to be seen in Delta County.)

Summer's role is ambiguous. Certainly no homesteader, he seems to have been a kind of hired (or perhaps voluntary) gun for the farmers. He was a crack shot with a rifle. Once, to demonstrate his skill, he shot a clay pipe from the lips of an unsuspecting passerby. Another time, in the Atkinson saloon, he shot off part of the tongue and some teeth of a man named Jerry Mahoney, who kept needling him about his infamous past.

The two men were friends of a sort, at least drinking buddies, but Summers had a violent temper and Mahoney's gibes finally got under his skin: "Jerry, your tongue is too long," he warned him. "Someday I'll shorten it for you." And he did.

After the shooting, Summers disappeared into the woods. A manhunt was organized but failed to capture him.

Several days previously, Summers and a friend named George Finch had gone fishing together in a small stream in a swamp a few miles south of town, riding there on a borrowed railroad handcar. The day after the shooting, Finch was handed a note addressed to him and delivered by one of the homesteaders. It had no signature, but Finch recognized the handwriting. It said: "George, do as we did Sunday, and be mum."

Finch got the homesteader to buy some food at the company store and that night went down the track on the handcar to deliver it to his friend. As he told it:

"When I reached the swamp, I heard a loud crashing noise in the brush and thought I was about to be eaten by wolves. I pumped the car as fast as I could for a while and about the time I was about to congratulate myself on my escape, I ran over pebbles or something that had been placed on the rails, and stopped so quickly the car left the track.

"As soon as the noise subsided, I heard heavy breathing and became desperately scared. "Is that you, George?" said Summers. And when I succeeded in answering, he said, "It's a good thing that it is you.

"I made several other trips to his hideout before leaving Atkinson, but I shall always remember that last night. We talked for hours before parting. Then he extended his thin cold hand, expressed gratitude for what I had done, bade me goodbye, and we parted—never to meet again."

The Atkinson mill was destroyed by fire in 1900; after that, the town languished and died. It was resuscitated in 1914, when lumberman Royal F. Gibbs built a sawmill on the south bank of the river just upstream from Atkinson. Some of the Atkinson buildings were moved there, and some former Atkinson workers were employed at the Gibbs mill and lumber camps. Following a familiar pattern, Atkinson had logged off the pine, and now Gibbs was harvesting the hardwood.

143

Gibbs City had a post office, granted in 1917, and a hotel-size boardinghouse accommodating up to two hundred people, along with other facilities and businesses. In 1922, its mill, too, was destroyed by an explosion. It had a brief renascence in 1941, when two big sawmills there produced hardwood lumber for army cots, powder boxes, and other wartime needs.

The old buildings stood empty for years after that. They were finally put to the torch in a controlled burning on April 13, 1966, at the behest of the property owners, who worried about people getting hurt there. Spectators came from miles around to watch the old town go up in smoke (a desecration to people like me) to the drumbeat of paint-can explosions and the popping of old bottles and electric light bulbs.

Now all that remains of Gibbs City are a few ruined foundations hidden in a jungle of weeds and brush. The only relic of Atkinson is the freestanding chimney of Ed Atkinson's home, in its day the biggest house in town.

27.

Manseau and the Old Gristmill

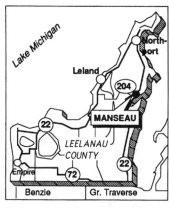

Manseau never got big enough to become a bona fide ghost town. But it had a siding on the old Traverse City Leelanau & Manistique Railroad, and it was a gathering place for Leelanau County farmers, who brought their grain to the gristmill for sale or to be ground for their own use.

The water-powered mill was built in 1859 by Antoine Manseau, Sr. In 1856, he had bought an acre of land on what he named Kenosha Creek from an Indian chief named Keywatosa for a hundred dollars. Three years later, he dammed the creek, built a 26' x 36' mill, and started grinding grain with a pair of imported millstones. They came from France, and were made of buhrstone, a

145

The Manseau Mill in the 1890's.

Lakeside view of the Manseau Mill, showing the dam and sluice gates.

The mill today.

One of the old millstones and marker on house lawn across the road from the mill.

composite of limestone and silica widely used for grindstones in those days.

The old mill building still stands on what is now called Belanger Creek, 3½ miles north of Suttons Bay. It probably is the oldest gristmill in the Grand Traverse area, antedating the Norris mill at Greilickville (now a residence) by at least two or three years.

Like his father, Antoine, Sr., Manseau was a millwright and carpenter. He was born in Canada, as was his father, and came to this country with the family in 1838. After spending some time in Green Bay, Milwaukee and

147

North Manitou Island, the Manseaus settled at the mouth of Carp River in Leelanau County. There, Manseau helped his father build a dam and sawmill on the river, thus founding the town of Leland in 1853.

In 1882, Antoine, Jr., built a 16' x 16' addition to his Kenosha Creek mill and installed the roller system necessary for milling flour. Even for today, that mill was a wonder of elaborate machinery of rollers, bolters and screens. The grain moved six times from basement to top floor, through three stands of rollers, four stands of silk bolters and screens that separated the coarse-ground bran and other products from the final fine-ground flour.

The mill was completely automatic. Only one man was needed to operate it—just to see that the grain kept moving in the right direction and to replace broken belts. There were fifty-two belts in the mill, and it is said that the experienced miller could tell by the sound exactly which one had broken.

In 1906, the mill was bought by Eugene Belanger and was operated by him and his sons Ignatius, Alexis, Luke and Edwin until 1934. By that time, very little grain was being raised in the Grand Traverse region, and the mill closed down because business was slow and the owners didn't want to spend the money for necessary repairs. Most Michigan grist mills also shut down around that time.

Ed Belanger remembers the mill's last day. He remembers it especially well because it was almost his last day, too. It was in the early spring of 1934, and he'd spent all day grinding grain for a local farmer. For most of that time, he and the farmer had stood on some planking over the seventeen-foot-deep water box that provided power for the mill wheels.

Ed went to a dance that night in Suttons Bay, and when he returned he found that part of the concrete wall of the water box had given way and the planking on which they had stood was a hundred yards out on the bay ice.

"If it had happened during that day," Ed says, "we'd both have been goners for sure."

The mill stands empty now, but the dam on Belanger Pond is still intact. The two original grinding stones are all that's left of the milling machinery.

Just north of the mill is a hillside where Suttons Bay's legendary hermit, Rock Tabeshevski, lived in a cave for several years around the turn of the century. Rock was a short, stocky, bewhiskered man with several layers of tattered clothing whose only companions were a cow and a bull and sometimes a calf. He called the bull "my boy" and the cow "my girl," and they were a familiar sight on the streets of Suttons Bay when he hitched them to a wagon and came to town for supplies at rare intervals.

Rock was a well-educated man; he spoke thirteen languages. It was said that he studied for the priesthood but then gave it up for a teaching job in Alpena. The story goes that he was doing penance for having unintentionally caused the death of one of his pupils, whom he punished too severely.

He died at the age of seventy-eight at the State Hospital in Traverse City.

28.

Walton Was a Hell of a Place

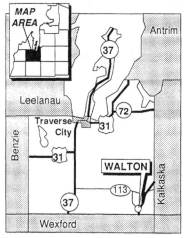

Hell was what they called it in the old lumbering days. Back then, if you asked any station agent on the Grand Rapids & Indiana Railroad for a ticket to hell, he'd hand you one to Walton without batting an eye.

Walton, also called Walton Junction, was a very tough town. Situated near the Grand Traverse-Wexford county line, it was the favorite watering hole and brawling place for lumberjacks and river hogs from rival camps along the Boardman and Manistee rivers—the only place between Traverse City and Cadillac where a thirsty man could buy a drink.

So they came to Walton by the hundreds whenever they couldn't work in the woods. After the evening trains came in and the lights began to glitter in Walton's three hotels,

150

ten saloons, and four bawdy houses, respectable people retired to the sanctuary of their homes and locked their doors. Barroom fights were commonplace, part of the entertainment. So nobody intervened when two lumberjacks fought by lamplight along the sawdust-strewn floor, battling for honor, reputation, rivalry, or just plain for the hell of it. Walton had no constable or sheriff to keep the peace, though some say it did have a jail at one time.

Walton got its start as a railroad junction in 1873, when the GR&I got that far on its way north to Petoskey and began building its branch line to Traverse City. A railroad construction foreman, A. F. Phillips, built the first house at Walton and kept boarders. Later he built the first hotel, the Grand Rapids & Indiana House. Walton qualified for a post office in 1873; its first postmaster was J. L. Gibbs, who later lived in Traverse City and was Grand Traverse County clerk. The two other early hotels were the Brownson House and the Walton House. A timber cruiser, H. A. Ferris, operated one of the first saloons. By 1880, Walton had a population of over a hundred.

One of Walton's most notorious "bad men" was Flip Gillespie, who worked as a bouncer in the Walton House bar, though it was said that nobody got bounced as long as he had enough money in his pockets to buy a drink. Flip got his nickname from the way he carried his six-shooter—slung low on his hip in western style—and flipped it out of the holster in a fast draw. He claimed he could outdraw and outshoot any man in six states, but he never had to prove it. Most lumberjacks carried no weapons except their fists and caulked boots.

Another legendary character who worked for a while on the Manistee River at Jam One (Sharon) and spent some time at Walton was Silver Jack Driscoll. A giant of a man at six-foot-four and whipcord-tough 180 pounds, Driscoll had the reputation of being the toughest, meanest, fightingest lumberjack of them all. It was said that when sober he could lick any man alive and when in his cups it took three of the very best to down him.

Jack drifted north with the lumbering and eventually worked in a logging camp in the Huron Mountains.

151

Walton was a junction for three railroads in the early 1900s.

General store at Walton, early 1900s.

Loading gravel on the Manistee & Northeastern Railroad at Walton. Early 1900s.

The cranberry marsh at Walton today.

The railroad tracks at Walton today.

He returned one day from a prospecting trip with a pocketful of silver nuggets (hence the nickname, Silver Jack) and told his friends that he planned to stake out a claim and make his fortune. He might have done it, too, except that he caught cold on a spring drive on the Yellow Dog River and died of pneumonia at the age of forty-one in a boardinghouse at L'Anse without divulging his secret.

Around 1880, a prominent Traverse City man, DeWitt Clinton Leach, publisher of the *Grand Traverse Herald,* started a cranberry farm in the big Walton marsh just west of the village. By 1900, it had become Walton's biggest industry. The annual crop of around 1,000 bushels was harvested by Indian pickers. On July 10, 1898, believe it or not, the entire crop was destroyed by a late frost.

Leach began his operation by building an earthen dam two hundred feet long across one end of the marsh. By means of a sluice gate he could regulate the water level to the lower part and make it suitable for cranberry cultivation. The dam created a shallow backup lake, on which Leach and his wife lived in a cottage for many years. The dam and the sluice gate and the lake are still there, but muskrats have tunneled through the ridges on which the cranberry bushes were planted and destroyed most of them.

Walton Junction acquired another railroad in 1910, when the Manistee & Northeastern built its River Branch from Kaleva to Grayling. The M&NE trains passed under the GR&I tracks through a deep ravine just north of the village. The MN&E grade is still visible, but the underpass was filled in years ago.

By 1920, Walton had begun its slow decline that coincided with the decline of railroad service. Now only one or two of the original houses remain and only one of the commercial buildings is still standing, and the old McManus Saloon, which was operated for years by George McManus. It used to face the railroad tracks, but in later years the entrance was changed to the rear. Until recent years, it served as a family residence.

29.

Peacock and the Legend of Bloody Run

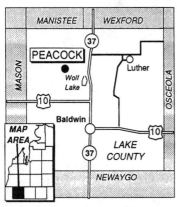

One thing that distinguishes Peacock from hundreds of other Michigan ghost towns that grew up along railroad tracks or around a sawmill is its black cemetery. It lies in the woods about half a mile east of town at the end of a sandy road appropriately marked "Dead End." (No pun, I feel sure, is intended.) Until just recently it was limited strictly to black people. Nobody else could get in.

This odd bit of reverse discrimination was the work of Alice Kelly, a white woman who came from New York State in the 1890s and bought up most of the land in and around Peacock. She also built the town's first hotel and livery stable. She had a husband but nobody seems

Peacock today is just a wide place in the road.

Pere Marquette depot at Peacock around 1890.

Concrete headstones in Peacock's black cemetery.

to know much about him, except that his name was George.

Peacock, like Baldwin and some other Lake County communities, had a sizable black population. Alice Kelly is said to have pitied them because they were so poor, and wanted to do something for them, so she gave them land for a burying ground.

The people who lie there must have been poor indeed, because all they could afford for a tombstone, most of them, was a concrete slab with the name and dates scratched in or painted on.

The ban against nonblacks was lifted recently and the cemetery is now racially integrated. This pleases some of the local white people who say they want to go there when the time comes.

Peacock was little more than a lumber camp and a logging-railroad stop on R. G. Peter's Manistee & Luther line until it got a boost in the early 1890s when another railroad, the Manistee & Grand Rapids (later Pere Marquette), came through on its way to Edgetts and

Manistee & Luther Railroad engine No. 3 with a train of logging flatcars on the high bridge across the Pine River near Peacock.

Tustin. The village was named for David J. Peacock, who became its first postmaster on April 15, 1897.

Firmly entrenched in village folklore is the Legend of Bloody Run. The tale has been handed down over the years, no doubt gaining in hyperbole with each retelling. The only written account was printed in a newspaper in 1939, half a century later, and it too is based entirely on hearsay. It goes something like this:

The place: a logging railroad siding on the Manistee & Luther line in the deep woods near Peacock. The time: a blustery cold winter day in 1886 or 1887.

A logging train is about to pull out with a heavy load of logs on a long string of flatcars, and a dozen or more lumberjacks are riding on the logs. The conductor gives the signal to start, but the engineer objects. It's too dangerous, he says. He points out to the conductor that the train must negotiate a 30 percent downhill grade to a small stream at the bottom and that the rails are slippery with snow and ice. What if the brakes don't hold?

The conductor isn't convinced, and a heated argument follows. Finally, the engineer in disgust climbs down from the cab, flatly refusing to budge. The conductor, in bravado or ignorance, takes his place in the cab. He moves the train out and it passes over the brink of the hill and down the slope. What happens then is just what the engineer had feared. Propelled by the heavily loaded flatcars, the little engine quickly gathers speed. The brakes fail to hold and all hell breaks loose.

The train goes bucketing, lurching, careening down the slippery tracks, out of control now and at breakneck speed. The engine derails and nose-dives into the riverbank, raising a great cloud of steam from its ruptured boiler. The flatcars buckle and crash into each other; some shedding their loads, are catapaulted into the air. The sky begins a rain of couplers and coupling pins, broken logging chains, car wheels, peavies, axes, pike poles and other debris—and the mangled bodies of lumberjacks. At least a score of them are killed, and the little stream, known to this day as Bloody Run, runs red with their blood.

The accident has never been documented. Did it really happen? Old-timers at Peacock say it did. That's how Bloody Run Creek got its name, they say. Anyway, they add, why let facts interfere with a good story?

30.

Crescent:
An Island Ghost Town

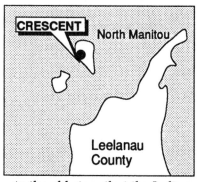

The Indians called them Manitou, meaning Great Spirit: to them the islands were sacred. Apparently, though, there's no truth to the old story that the Indians avoided the islands because they were thought to harbor evil spirits.

North and South Manitou Islands lie some twelve miles offshore from the Leelanau County peninsula. They were once part of Manitou County, which went out of existence in 1895, when the two islands became part of Leelanau County.

Now also a part of the Sleeping Bear Dunes National Lakeshore and virtually unpopulated, the islands have a long, interesting history, and many people once called them home. They were familiar landmarks to the earliest travelers on Lake Michigan: first the Indians, then

French traders, trappers, missionaries and explorers, as early as the second half of the seventeenth century.

And the earliest white settlers in the Grand Traverse region came first to the Manitous—to South Manitou about 1835 and to its neighbor just a few years later. Some stayed and some moved on.

In 1846, brothers Nicholas and Simeon Pickard built a pier, set up a wooding station on the east shore of North Manitou, and began selling hardwood, in four-foot lengths and split, to fuel the boilers of passing lake steamers on the Chicago-Buffalo run. Two or three families of woodcutters were already living there.

Eight years later, Simeon Pickard established another wooding station on the west side of the island and started the village of Crescent. It lay on a shallow bay that's shaped like a crescent moon. Later on, he also built a small sawmill there.

For a long time the settlement didn't amount to much: just a few families of woodcutters and fishermen. But it began to flourish soon after the turn of the century.

In 1906, two Traverse City lumbermen, W. Cary Hull and Frank H. Smith, bought large tracts of timberland on the island and prepared to log off one of the last great stands of virgin timber in the region. Hull was the son of Henry Hull, president and founder of Oval Wood Dish Company, Traverse City's biggest manufacturer; Smith was a timber cruiser for that firm.

During the next three years, Smith and Hull built a long dock and a big sawmill and other company buildings at Crescent, and completed five miles of standard-gauge logging railroad into the woods. In 1909, they began logging operations on a big scale, hauling the first load of logs to the mill on July 12 with a secondhand Shay locomotive (No. 3) and twelve Russell logging cars. The rolling stock was shipped to Crescent from Muskegon aboard the steam barge *J. O. Nessen.*

Later that year, they bought a second, brand-new Shay engine (No. 1) and built three more miles of track. The engine was shipped by rail to Frankfort, then carried to Crescent on a barge.

Schoolhouse at Crescent on North Manitou Island, 1910.

Smith and Hull dock at Crescent harbor on North Manitou Island.

Smith & Hull's Shay locomotive No. 1 hauling logs to Crescent.

Schooner *Stafford* anchored near Crescent in 1909. The boat took on a cargo of hemlock bark for tanneries in Milwaukee.

The company figured that the logging operation would take six years. The sawmill could turn out forty thousand board feet of lumber a day. It was loaded on ships waiting at the dock and carried to markets in Chicago and Detroit. It is said that the ships loading lumber at the company's six hundred-foot dock averaged one a day in season.

Esther Morse of Lake Ann went from Cedar Run with her family to live at Crescent in 1908. She was seven years old. Her father, Andrew J. White, and her brother, James, ran the sawmill.

She remembers a lot about the town, remembers going to school that first year in a tiny building next to the saloon. Her cousin, Mary Cate, was the teacher. She instructed her pupils to address her as Miss Cate, and was visibly annoyed when Esther sometimes slipped and called her just plain Mary. She was a little strict at first, Esther says, but mellowed some, after a while. Belle Halvorsen taught at the school later.

The village went dry in the following year, ousting the saloon as a bad influence, and the school moved into the much larger saloon building. Esther Morse thinks that may be one for the books: school takes over saloon. Sunday school classes were also held there, as were Sunday church services, Reverend Babcock officiating.

Esther also remembers, only too well, the bad day when her father was injured in an accident at the mill. He was underneath the "bull chain" (which pulled the logs from the millpond into the mill), oiling a bearing, when his sleeve got caught in the moving chain and his left arm was drawn into the machinery and mutilated.

The arm had to be amputated, and Dr. Edwin Thirlby was brought from Traverse City by boat for the operation, which he performed on the family dining room table with the assistance of the local doctor. Esther had been sent to the boardinghouse next door, but says she watched part of the operation through a window.

At its peak, from 1908 to 1915, some three hundred people lived at Crescent. Besides the sawmill, the town had a big general store, post office (in the store), schoolhouse, and a boardinghouse where the single mill hands lived. The loggers had their quarters in the woods, at some distance from the town. Phil Thiel ran the general store; Frank A. Dean was the first postmaster, in 1908. The big mill provided electricity for the town.

Esther Morse also remembers the sad day of July 5, 1915. That was the day all the mill machinery was loaded aboard the schooner *J. O. Nessen,* and she sailed away, carrying almost everything that made the sawmill a sawmill and Crescent a town. The railroad's rolling stock and rails were removed sometime later.

A few people lingered for a while. But most of the residents moved across to a settlement on the east side of the island, and to the mainland, and it wasn't long before the village was completely deserted.

Now all that's left is a big old barn built in 1925, the concrete foundations for the mill's steam engine, a few spiles of the old dock, and miles of railroad bed running through the woods from nowhere to nowhere.

31.

Stratford Nearly Disappeared

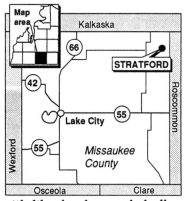

Many Michigan ghost towns have vanished almost without a trace. Nothing is left except maybe an open field with lilac bushes and shallow depressions in the ground where houses (and outhouses) once stood. Abandoned buildings go to pieces pretty fast in Michigan's damp climate. It isn't like the Far West, where whole villages may remain intact for decades, preserved in the dry desert air.

For this reason, and others, Stratford, in the northeast corner of Missaukee County, is one of Michigan's most satisfactory ghost towns.

Signs show you where everything was: The Depot, Main Line, Wye Track, General Store, The Hotel, Smith & Hull grade, and so on. A larger sign between two posts at roadside on the Moorestown Road offers a capsule history of the old village.

All this was the work of Michigan's Department of Conservation, which acquired the site in 1937 and sought to preserve it, or at least the memory of it, for posterity.

Stratford, like Deward in Crawford County, was a company town, first, last and always. The company built the town as headquarters for its logging operations, and when the timber was gone they packed it up and moved away. The timber—and the town—lasted twelve years. Along with Deward, which was logged off at about the same time, Stratford marked the end of big pine logging days in Lower Michigan.

In 1897, the Thayer Lumber Company of Muskegon bought 13,400 acres of timber in the Stratford area and began logging operations on a grand scale with the latest in machinery and equipment. Their timber holding at Stratford was one of the only two big stands of virgin white and red pine left in Lower Michigan; the other was at Deward.

That same year, the Pere Marquette Railroad extended its Rapid City branch from Kalkaska to Stratford primarily to accommodate the Thayer Company. During the next twelve years, from 1897 to 1908, the railroad hauled an average of thirty-six carloads of logs each day, six days a week, from Stratford to the Thayer mills at Muskegon. The company employed 150 men year-around and cut about 40 million board feet annually. All told, they took out an estimated 450 million board feet, and other companies along the thirty-two mile stretch of railroad—Stearns, Dempsey, Butcher, and others—probably harvested as many more.

Among the latter was Smith & Hull, a Traverse City firm. They built a standard-gauge logging railroad into the woods from Stratford and hauled logs to the Pere Marquette Railroad with their Shay locomotive, probably the same one of the two they would use to log off North Manitou Island in 1909.

Pere Marquette Railroad No. 176 about to leave Thayer
Lumber Company's camp at Stratford with a load of pine logs.

Pere Marquette engine No. 119 at Stratford Depot, early 1900s.

In its efforts to preserve the memory of Stratford by marking out the sites, the Department of Conservation was helped immeasurably by Fred Hirzel of Moorestown. Fred was a young man in 1937, and he remembered Stratford very well. His father owned the general store in Moorestown, and Fred delivered beef, butter, and eggs to the logging village.

According to Hirzel, there were two men's shanties for seventy-five men each. The fifteen houses were homes

Michigan DNR sign at Stratford.

The author at the Stratford village site in 1991.

for the railroad employees, company men with families, and village business owners. Two big log barns sheltered twenty teams of horses, and another building housed two hundred head of hogs.

There was a long cook shanty, a blacksmith shop, a general store, a hotel and several saloons. The railroad depot was the busiest place in town. Fred said he counted as many as nine locomotives in the village at one time. One Pere Marquette passenger train came into town every day, and for a dollar you could ride to Traverse City or Petoskey. The crew of the passenger train called it the "Klondike Branch" because the winters were so awful.

The Western Union Telegraph and Cable Company's office was at the depot. "This was the first time we knew what time it was" Hirzel said. "Before then we had to go into Lake City to get the correct time. They got it every day at eleven o'clock from Chicago."

Fred Hirzel became known as an authority of Michigan's lumbering era. During the course of a long and busy life, he acquired a marvelous collection of logging and railroad photographs, many of which he took himself. Like the C. T. Stoner Collection at the University of Michigan's Bentley Library, the Hirzel Collection is a priceless heritage from old logging days in Michigan.

32.
Show Me the Way
To Jacktown

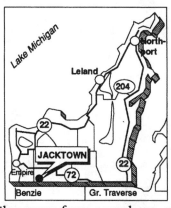

(The following is a fiction account of one of the many Jacktown legends.) We were out in the boon docks hunting grouse, miles away from anywhere, when we seen this old guy coming down the two-track. He had long white hair and he was almost as thin as the walking stick he'd picked up in the woods somewhere. We were parked a little ways off the trail, and I think he would have gone right by without ever seeing us, but Bert says, not loud, "Hello, there," and he give a start.

"Hello," he said, and come walking over.

"Where are you headed?" Bert asked him.

"I'm looking for Jacktown," the old guy says. "Can you tell me the way to Jacktown?"

"Jacktown!" Bert says.

Dead elm tree at Jacktown, railroad grade at rear.

The Bland cemetery at Jacktown.

"Yes," the old guy say. "It's a little place called Jacktown. Maybe you have heard of it."

"Oh, I heard of it, all right," Bert says slowly, like he thinks maybe the old guy is trying to pull his leg. "Jacktown."

"Can you show me how to get there?"

"How long has it been since you were there?" Bert asked him.

"Oh, not long," he says. "It's been a while but not too long. The trouble is, everything seems changed. I don't recognize anything anymore. Things are different from the way I remember."

"That's only natural," Bert says. "But where do you live now?"

"I live at Jacktown," the old guy says.

Grave of Mary Wakefield (no relation to author) in Bland cemetery.

Bert looked at him.

"You live at Jacktown," Bert said. "All right. I can show you the way. But I think you ought to know that there's not much left of it anymore. In fact, there ain't nothing left of it. It's what they call a ghost town. But I don't think there's even a ghost there now. Nobody's lived there for almost fifty years."

"Is that so?" the old man says, but you could see he hadn't even been listening. "I live right near the railroad tracks," he said. "Just a little way from the station."

"Sure," Bert said. "The old Empire and Southeastern. They used to call it 'Empire slow and easy' or 'Empire and something else.' But the railroad doesn't go there anymore. They took up the tracks at least thirty years ago, during the war when metal was scarce. They even took up the ties. The railroad's gone. Just like the town."

"I expect there's been some change," the old man said, absently.

"You wouldn't believe how much," Bert said.

The old man looked at him—smiling, expectant, eager. "I'd sure like to get there before dark. Can you show me the way? I must have taken a wrong turn back there." He took out a bandanna and wiped the sweat from his long thin face. It was a warm day in late September. The maple leaves had just started to turn—red, orange and yellow at the tips. The old man's eyes were light blue.

"Sure," Bert said. "We'll do better than that. We'll take you there."

The old man smiled. "I'd be much obliged. But I don't want to put you to any trouble."

"No trouble at all," Bert said cheerfully. "Don't you give it a thought."

So we all got into the pickup and Bert started off down the woods trail. I guess it was about two miles from there to Jacktown, and I didn't remember the way exactly, but Bert did, and we had to do a lot of twisting and turning before we got there. I knew where we were when we started down that long wooded slope and into the open valley where Jacktown used to be. You could see the old railroad bed snaking along through it, but as Bert said, they'd taken up the rails a long time ago. Even the ties were gone.

"Well, here we are," Bert said. "This is Jacktown. What's left of it."

We all got out and looked around. There wasn't much to see. You could tell where the train station had been, but it was all grown up in weeds. Down in the middle of the open valley was the skeleton of a big old elm tree, dead limbs scattered around the base of it.

The old man looked bewildered. "Are you sure this is the place?"

"Yes," Bert said. "This is Jacktown. That's what they used to call it. Can you remember where you lived?"

The old man shook his head. "I don't know," he said. "I can't remember."

Bert pointed to a clump of lilac bushes at the top of a little knoll not far from where the train station used to be. "There's an old foundation up there," he said. "Do you want to take a look?"

The old man nodded. We walked up there. The ruined concrete-and-cobblestone foundation of a house was hidden by lilac bushes all around. There was a big cellar, filled now with all kinds of rubble and junk. The old man looked down into it blankly. He didn't say anything. Then he bent down and picked up a rusty piece of metal, an old door hinge. He looked at it wonderingly, turning it over in his hand, then dropped it into the hole.

I realize now that we should have taken him back to town. It was at least fifteen miles and he couldn't ever have made it before dark. But he wouldn't go. He said he wanted to hang around there for a while. He said not to worry, he'd be all right. We argued but he wouldn't budge.

We didn't feel right about it, we felt uneasy about it, but short of picking him up bodily and putting him in the truck, there wasn't anything we could do. He was a gentle old man. We didn't want to rough him up.

On the way back to town Bert turns to me and says, "Are you thinking the same thing I'm thinking?"

"What's that?"

"Rip Van Winkle."

"Ah, come on now. You serious?"

"I don't know," he said.

But then I thought about it for a while and started laughing and we both had a good laugh over it. But we were worried too, and next day we drove back out there and looked all over for him. There were some other old cellar holes and we looked in all of them. We looked all over the fields. We looked in the woods. But we didn't find him. We didn't find hide nor hair of him.

A day or two later we read in the paper that one of the patients was missing from the State Hospital. They figured he'd just wandered off somewhere. From the description in the paper we knew it must be the old man—our old man at Jacktown. We kept checking the paper to see if there was any more news of him, but there wasn't any. He had just disappeared. They couldn't find a trace of him, Either somebody—like us—had picked him up or he had died of exposure somewhere in the woods.

Then a friend of Bert's who works at the State Hospital told him the old man's story. He'd been a patient at the asylum for fifty years or more. They said he lost his mind when his young wife died in childbirth. The baby died too. He couldn't handle the grief. He went out of his head and began to do strange things, so they had to lock him up. He wasn't violent—never had been, but he was way out of it. His name was Oliver Bland.

It was almost two months later, during deer hunting season, when they found him. He'd been dead a long time. There's an old cemetery out there—they call it the Bland Cemetery, because there's other Blands buried there; most of them are Blands. It has a rusty wrought iron fence around it, and it must have been pretty nice in the old days, but now it's chock full of weeds and brush. There are the graves of some of the people who used to live at Jacktown. Most of the people just moved away. The story is that suddenly one summer all the wells went dry.

During deer season in November a hunter happened to look in there and saw something that didn't look right. It was a cold day and there was about two inches of snow on the ground. He saw something dark in there and went in to investigate. He thought it might be a dead deer.

The old man was lying across one of the graves. He was just lying there like he was sleeping. He looked comfortable, peaceful. The headstone was covered with moss and mold, but the hunter scraped it away with his knife, and here is what he read:

To the Memory of
Thelma Bland
Beloved Wife of Oliver Bland
1890-1910

But that was all right. There was nothing bad about that. Because any way you want to figure it, see, the old man had come home. He was home free at last.

There was an inscription on the other side of the stone, too. Somebody said it was from a poem by Longfellow.

There is a Reaper whose
Name is Death,
And with his sickle keen,
He reaps the bearded
grain at a breath,
And the flowers that
grow between.

33.

Looking For Goo

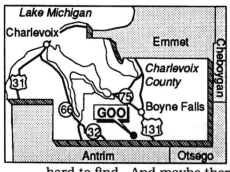

After all the trouble I had finding Tunk, I never thought I'd really go looking for Goo. Goo seemed too remote, too hard to find. And maybe there wasn't anything left of it, so how would I know when I got there?

Goo and Tunk were railroad stops listed in a book called *Along the Tracks: A Directory of Named places on Michigan Railroads,* by Graydon M. Meints. The names intrigued me. Tunk was a siding on the old Pere Marquette Railroad in Grand Traverse County near Mabel. Goo was a timber stop on the south branch of the Boyne City Railroad in Charlevoix County. Both railroads have long since gone out of existence.

Meints lists range, township and section coordinates for Tunk, making it relatively easy to find. But Goo is a mystery. Even he doesn't know exactly where it is.

Compounding the problem is that there's no good map of the Boyne City Railroad. So you can understand my reluctance to go off on what might turn out to be a wild Goo chase.

But you know how it is: Goo was a challenge. It kept popping up in my mind. After a while it became an obsession. So one day I said to my wife, a breathtakingly practical girl who nonetheless shares my love of adventure and is often kind enough to overlook my aberrations, "Let's go find Goo." She was willing, so we hopped in the car and headed north.

I had solved part of the problem by coordinating a rough sketch map of the Boyne City Railroad dated 1906 with an excellent, detailed map of Charlevoix County published by the Michigan Department of Natural Resources (DNR) in 1960. According to my calculations, Goo must lie near Warner Creek in Section 31, Boyne Valley Township, Charlevoix County. (Meints puts it in Antrim County, but I think he's mistaken.)

Section 31 is a wilderness: no roads into it, paved or otherwise. But the DNR map shows a two-track that looked promising; it was an extension of Rogers Road, a mile and a half south of Deer Lake.

But the two-track was gone. We couldn't find a trace of it. Nobody was at home in the only nearby farm, and it was getting late. So Goo would have to wait until another day. I figured we'd come within a half mile of it. Close, but no cigar.

A couple of weeks went by before we had another shot. This time we decided to attack from the east. The DNR map shows another two-track a mile west of U.S. 131 on Renke Road, two miles south of Boyne Falls. The two-track leads into the heart of Section 31 and beyond. If it was still there, I figured we had it made.

In 1903, the Boyne City Railroad opened a southern branch into Antrim County. It ran south to Moore and Project. Here it branched again, one line running southeast to Camp 10, the other southwest to Goo. At Goo there was another Y, one branch going due south to

179

Old Boyne City Railroad grade runs high and dry through a mile of cedar swamp.

Site of the "Y" switch at Goo today.

The site of
Little John's Mill,
half mile east
of Goo.

Poster of the W.D.
Goo & Co.,
Boyne Falls, 1900.

WANTED!

1,000,000 Feet of Elm and Basswood Logs

AND

2,000 Cords 18 Inch Basswood Bolts.

We Will Pay The Highest Market Price On Cars Or In Our Yards.

LIBERAL ADVANCES

On Logs ON Skids In Woods When Required.

Lengths for Basswood Logs 12, 14, 16 feet. Lengths for Elm Logs 5 feet 3 inches, 10 feet 6 inches, 16 feet.

W. D. Goo & Co.

BOYNE FALLS, Dec. 18, 1900.

Brown, Dow, Kentucky, and other stops in Antrim County, the other southwest to Windling. All these tiny settlements along the railroad long ago vanished without a trace.

But the two-track was still there. It soon became obvious that it was a part of the old railroad grade. It runs on a beeline, high and dry, through a mile of cedar swamp. After crossing three branches of Collins Creek, it comes to a large clearing on higher ground and a sign that reads: Little John's Mill 1906. The sign is hand-lettered on the rusty blade of an old mill saw, mounted on a big wooden cross.

Goo lies in another clearing half a mile farther on.

Here, still in plain view (though of course the tracks and ties are gone) is the Y. One branch leads on to the southwest, the other makes a sharp turn south. Except for a few other vestiges of old logging days—grey twisted hulks of discarded logs, traces of the skidways where logs were piled—nothing else remains. Sand-and-pebble-bottom Warner Creek runs along the west side of the clearing, its water as clear as Holland gin.

Later I talked with the farmer who owns most of Section 31. Goo lies on the northeast corner of his back forty.

"We always called it Goo switch," he told me.

But he didn't know the answer to one question that still bugs me, nor did any of a half dozen other old-timers I interviewed in the area:

Where did Goo get its name? Why did they call it Goo?

Alas, we may never know.

The story of Goo appeared in the July 27, 1990, issue of the *Traverse City Record-Eagle's Summer Magazine.* Almost a year later, I received a letter from Bernard S. Kondrat, Sr., of Boyne Falls, Michigan. He enclosed a copy of the "wanted" poster shown here, which makes it clear that Goo was named for W. D. Goo of a lumber company of that name in Boyne Falls. Mr. Kondrat's letter is worth quoting in full:

June 30, 1991

Dear Mr. Wakefield:

In the July 27, 1990, issue, a friend of mine, Emerald Magee from Traverse City brought me the paper. I live on Renke Road just a little way from Goo Switch. My Grandfather & Father used to tell me about Goo Logging & Sawmill & Railroad. Thirty-eight years ago we bought an old house in Boyne Falls & found this wanted poster I am sending you.

I was born & raised on Renke Road. Used to walk after cows in the evening towards Goo Switch. On the two-track road we used to catch Brook Trout when I was a little boy.

Yours truly, Benard S. Kondrat, Sr.

Thanks to Mr. Kondrat, the mystery is finally solved.